# WORDS OF LOVE

MARK RUTKOSKI

TRENCHART: SURPLUS

∮

LES FIGUES PRESS
Los Angeles

Design & typsetting: Emma Williams

Words of Love
FIRST EDITION

ISBN 13: 978-1-934254-39-4
ISBN 10: 1-934254-39-8
Library of Congress Control Number: 2012948829

Source: William Shakespeare, *Complete Sonnets (Unabridged)*, New York: Dover Publications, Inc. (Dover Thrift Editions), 1991 (containing the complete text of the Sonnets from *The Poems of William Shakespeare*, Black's Readers Service Company, New York, n.d.).

Les Figues Press thanks its subscribers for their support and readership. Les Figues Press is a 501c3 organization. Donations are tax-deductible.

Les Figues would like to acknowledge the following individuals for their generosity: Peter Binkow and Johanna Blakley, Lauren Bon, Chris and Diane Calkins, and Coco Owen.

Les Figues Press titles are available through:
Les Figues Press, <http://www.lesfigues.com>
Small Press Distribution, <http://www.spdbooks.org>

Special thanks to Erin Kilduff and Militza Jean-Felix.

TrenchArt 7/3

Book 4 of 6 in the TRENCHART Surplus Series.

This project is supported in part by a generous grant from the National Endowment of the Arts.

ART WORKS.
arts.gov

LES FIGUES PRESS

Post Office Box 7736
Los Angeles, CA 90007
323.734.4732 / info@lesfigues.com
www.lesfigues.com

# CONTENTS

# EXAKTE WISSENSCHAFT UND/ALS POESIE

Annette Gilbert

"I offer you a Shakespeare sonnet, but it is no longer his."
Tom Stoppard *Travesties*

Wenn die Figur Tristan Tzara in Tom Stoppards *Travesties* (1975) Shakespeares 18. Sonett zerschneidet, um zu zeigen, dass man aus diesem Sonett unzählige andere Liebessonette machen und seiner Liebsten darbieten kann, so ist dies eine eher harmlose Parodie, zumal sie sich im Rahmen der Fiktion bewegt. Um was aber handelt es sich, wenn Mark Rutkoski für *Words of Love* tatsächlich alle Sonette Shakespeares in ihre einzelnen Wörter 'zerschneidet', alphabetisch anordnet und als eigenständiges Werk unter seinem Namen veröffentlicht? Um Dichtung? Eher mag man an quantitative Grundlagenforschung für die Shakespeare-Forschung denken. Doch wozu? Die Literaturwissenschaft ist mit etwa 100 Referenzwerken zu Shakespeare, darunter etlichen statistischen, bereits bestens versorgt. Schon 1874 legte Horace Howard Furness *A Concordance to Shakespeare's Poems. An Index to Every Word therein Contained* vor; 1968 folgte Martin Spevacks mit Hilfe der ersten Computer angefertigte *A Complete and Systematic Concordance to the Works of Shakespeare*. Zwar haben statistische Textanalysen mit den Digital Humanities jüngst neuen Auftrieb erfahren. Doch ist im digitalen Zeitalter der *Druck* einer neuen Konkordanz völlig

# EXACT RESEARCH AND/AS POETRY

Translated by Vivien Knussi

"I offer you a Shakespeare sonnet, but it is no longer his."
Tom Stoppard *Travesties*

When the character Tristan Tzara in Tom Stoppard's *Travesties* (1975) cuts up Shakespeare's 18th sonnet in order to make a new one, he shows that he likewise can make numerous others for his lover. The gesture can be seen as a harmless parody because it remains within the boundary of fiction. But what happens when Mark Rutkoski in *Words of Love* literally "cuts up" the Shakespeare sonnets into their constituent words, alphabetizes them and publishes this as an autonomous work of art? Is it poetry? Rather, one might think of the basic quantitative research in Shakespeare studies. But why bother? The scholarly literature on Shakespeare is already well supplied with many statistical reference works, including *A Concordance to Shakespeare's Poems: An Index to Every Word therein Contained* published by Horace Howard Furness in 1874 and the first computer-made *A Complete and Systematic Concordance to the Works of Shakespeare* by Martin Spevacks in 1968. Nevertheless, there is new enthusiasm in the humanities for digital statistical text analysis. However, in the digital age printing a new concordance is obsolete, with databases and websites allowing for much more individualized, flexible and complex analyses.

obsolet, erlauben einschlägige Datenbanken und Internetseiten doch viel individuellere, flexiblere und komplexere statistische Textauswertungen als jede gedruckte Konkordanz.

Hinzu kommt, dass der Nutzen dieser Forschung zwar für die Sprachwissenschaft auf der Hand liegt, der sie Rohdaten für weiterführende lexikographische, sprachstilistische und -historische Untersuchungen und Lexika liefert. Ihr konkreter literaturwissenschaftlicher Erkenntnisgewinn ist allerdings noch immer recht umstritten, sieht man von Stil-, Genre- und Autorschaftsbestimmungen ab. Oft scheint man aus den Statistiken doch nur zu erfahren, was man auch vorher schon ahnte: Etwa dass Shakespeares Sonette quantitativ von Funktionswörtern wie "and", "the", "to", "of", "in", "that" dominiert werden, dass "love" das meistgebrauchte Inhaltswort ist, dass Shakespeare die petrarkistische Tradition mit neuen Bildern aus dem Handels- und Bankenwesen, der Jurisprudenz und dem Theater angereichert hat oder dass "I" und alle zugehörigen Formen die größte Wortgruppe bilden.

Sicher, der letzte Befund mag einen Ansatz zur Erklärung der biographistisch geprägten Rezeptionsgeschichte der Sonette bieten, die bekanntlich erst relativ spät von den Romantikern als Meisterwerk innerhalb des Shakespeareschen Oeuvres und der Weltliteratur entdeckt und gewürdigt worden waren, dabei aber in einem unzulässigen Kurzschluss von lyrischem Ich und Autor als 'romantische Erlebnislyrik' – als "Schlüssel, mit dem Shakespeare [uns] sein Herz aufschließt" (Wordsworth) – missverstanden wurden. In der Folge waren es vor allem die biographischen Ungereimtheiten statt der intrinsischen poetischen Qualitäten, die den

The need for this linguistic research is obvious; it provides the raw data for further lexicographic, stylistic, and historical studies. Apart from issues of style, genre, and authorship, however, their insights for literary studies are still debatable. Often it seems statistics merely confirm what one thought to be true of Shakespeare's sonnets: that the quantity of function words such as "and," "the," "to," "of," "in," "that" predominate; that "love" is the most widely used content word; that Shakespeare has enriched the Petrarchan tradition with new images from trading and banking, the law and the theater; or that "I" and all of its forms makes up the largest group of words.

Sure, the latter finding may be an approach to explain the markedly biographically-driven reception history has offered the sonnets, which were recognized relatively late by the Romantics as a masterpiece within Shakespeare's oeuvre and world literature. Yet, the lyrical "I" has been misunderstood and mistaken for the author – as if Shakespeare himself was speaking in the sonnets – as in "with this key Shakespeare unlocked his heart" (Wordsworth). Consequently, the biographical inconsistencies rather than the intrinsic poetic qualities kept the sonnet cycle in discussion. This repeatedly elicited new experiments to identify the characters with real people, and caused the regrouping of the seemingly disordered 154 sonnets.

But as Stéphane Mallarmé once so aptly remarked, it is not with ideas that poems are made, but with words. It is this linguistic dimension of the sonnets that Mark Rutkoski's index helps to right. However, such a listing of verbal material is not indicative of the real secret of poetry. So how were these 'normal' and now often perceived as worn-out words (see the entrance theme of The Mamas

Sonettzyklus im Gespräch hielten und immer wieder neue Versuche der Identifikation der Figuren mit realen Personen und der Neugruppierung der merkwürdig ungeordnet erscheinenden 154 Sonette hervorriefen.

Dabei sind es doch, wie Stéphane Mallarmé einst so treffend formulierte, die Worte und nicht die Ideen, aus denen Gedichte gemacht werden. Eben dieser sprachlichen Dimension der Sonette verhilft Mark Rutkoski mit seinem Index wieder zu ihrem Recht. Allerdings gibt ein solche Auflistung des reinen Wortmaterials keinerlei Aufschluss über das eigentliche Geheimnis der Poesie, also darüber, wie sich diese ganz 'normalen' und inzwischen – folgt man dem Eingangsmotto von The Mamas and the Papas – häufig als schal empfundenen Wörter wie "love", "sweet", "beauty", "eyes" und "heart" unter Shakespeares ingeniöser Feder zu einem der bewundertesten Werke der Weltliteratur zusammenfügen.

Ebenso wenig nutzt Rutkoski hier das analysierte Sprachmaterial zur Generierung neuer Texte, wie es in der experimentellen Literatur (und auch in seinem eigenem Oeuvre, wo er häufig eine bestimmte Anzahl von Elementen mithilfe mathematischer Methoden kombiniert) nicht selten der Fall ist. Erinnert sei nur an die auf Anregung Max Benses entstandenen *Stochastischen Texte* von Theo Lutz (1959), die auf einem *Zuse Z22* aus dem Wortschatz von Franz Kafkas *Das Schloß* erzeugt wurden, oder an Emmett Williams' Poem *musica* (1968), das die neun häufigsten Wörter der *Divina Commedia* so oft wiederholt, wie sie in Dantes Werk erscheinen. Aus jüngerer Zeit sei Charles Bernsteins Poem *I and the* (1986) genannt, dessen Dreizeiler sich aus den häufigsten Wörtern laut Hartvig Dahls *Word Frequencies in Spoken American English* zusammensetzen.

and the Papas) like "love," "sweet," "beauty," "eyes" and "heart" transformed by Shakespeare's ingenious pen to become one of the most admired works of world literature?

Rutkoski's analysis here does not use the language material to generate new texts, as is often the case in experimental literature (although in his own oeuvre, he often combines a number of elements using mathematical methods). One need only recall the resulting texts suggested by Max Bense such as Theo Lutz's *Stochastic Text* (1959), which was generated on a *Zuse Z22* computer from the vocabulary of Franz Kafka's *The Castle*, or Emmett Williams's poem *Musica* (1968) based upon the most common words in Dante's *Divine Comedy*. Or, more recently, Charles Bernstein's poem with three-line stanzas *I and the* (1986), composed from the words appearing most often in Hartvig Dahl's *Word Frequencies in Spoken American English*.

Instead Rutkoski simply left *Words of Love* as an index, publishing it under his name and claiming it as an autonomous work of art, which has to be mildly irritating especially given the call for originality in Western art and literature. But dealing with a classic in such a way is not as unusual as it may seem – especially in the context of conceptual writing and appropriation. In fact it has become an almost common artistic response to the digital age (considering the rising tide of produced and accessible texts and the changing approach to texts and intellectual property). There are even connections to a number of works, such as Simon Popper's alphabetized *Ulysses* (2006); Karen Reimer's and Sally Alatalo's romantic dime novel *Legendary, Lexical, Loquacious Love* (1996); Leïla Brett's *À la recherche du temps perdu I, Index* (2004); and Nick Thurston's *Historia Abscondita (An Index of Joy)* (2007). These all turn into reality

Dass es Rutkoski bei der Erstellung eines Indexes belässt, diesen als *Words of Love* unter seinem Namen veröffentlicht und so als eigenständiges künstlerisches Werk für sich reklamiert, dürfte daher zumindest irritieren. Im Kontext von Conceptual Writing und Appropriation Literature ist dieser demonstrativ das Originalitätsdiktat unserer westlichen Kultur unterwandernde Umgang mit einem Klassiker allerdings nicht ungewöhnlich und als geradezu typische künstlerische Reaktion auf die mediengeschichtliche Zäsur des digitalen Zeitalters (d.h. auf die wachsende Flut an produzierten und zugänglichen Texten und auf den sich ändernden Umgang mit Texten und mit geistigem Eigentum) zu werten. Anschlüsse ergeben sich so zu einer Reihe ähnlicher Arbeiten, etwa zu Simon Poppers alphabetisiertem *Ulysses* (2006), Karen Reimers und Sally Alatalos alphabetisiertem Dreigroschenroman *Legendary, Lexical, Loquacious Love* (1996) oder den Indexarbeiten von Leïla Brett *À la recherche du temps perdu I. Index* (2004) und Nick Thurston *Historia Abscondita (An Index of Joy)* (2007). Sie alle setzen die einst von Jorge Luis Borges in *Pierre Menard, Autor des Quijote* (1939) entworfene Fiktion in die Realität um.

Dabei wollen derartige Alphabetisierungen und Indexe nicht wie eine gewöhnliche Konkordanz lediglich *konsultiert*, sondern tatsächlich *gelesen* werden. Ein deutlicher Hinweis darauf ist, dass Rutkoski die billige Volksausgabe der Dover Thrift Editions *Complete Sonnets Unabridged* von 1991 zur Textgrundlage wählt, die wissenschaftlichen Ansprüchen natürlich nicht genügt. In starkem Kontrast zu den wenig ansprechenden Computerausdrucken der wissenschaftlichen Konkordanzen steht zudem die typographische Ästhetik seines Indexes. Und schließlich bringt Rutkoski weder den Kontext der Fundstellen noch kennzeichnet er Homonyme und die verschiedenen what Jorge Luis Borges once conceived of in his *Pierre Menard, Author of the Quixote* (1939).

These alphabetizations and indices are not to be *consulted* merely as one does an ordinary concordance, but are actually to be *read*. A clear indication is that Rutkoski chose the cheap and popular Dover Thrift Editions *Complete Sonnets Unabridged* text of 1991 as the textual basis for his work, which does not satisfy scholarly requirements. In stark contrast to the less appealing computer printouts of a traditional concordance is the aesthetic typography of his index. And finally, Rutkoski does not provide the context for the references, nor does he identify homonyms and the various forms of words, and neither does he quantify their exact frequencies. Instead he simply lists all occurrences of each word together and makes its frequency apparent at a glance. Since the columns act as the graph of a chart, depending on the word, they extend to different widths, which are at the same time the 'measured' word lengths. Out of these countless repetitions numerous patterns keep emerging. For example on the "I" pages, they all but eliminate the meaning of the letters as they fade into the background.

Due to this arrangement, the strict sonnet form is transferred with its end rhymes in a vertical structure, which, with its alliterative effects, recalls sound poetry and Dadaist nonsense, like "you ye you your" in Kurt Schwitters's *Anna Blume*. Nevertheless, even in these phrases it is not rare to encounter surprising sense. This is probably due to the ineradicable potential of language to generate sense and our irrepressible urge to find meaning through reading. In addition, of course you can read the index columns in various directions: vertically line by line ("annoy anon anon another") or even horizontally across the page ("Eve's eye eyes face" and "tongues translate true truth ugly").

Wortformen noch beziffert er die exakten Häufigkeiten. Stattdessen reiht er einfach alle Vorkommnisse jedes Worts aneinander und macht dergestalt die Häufigkeitsverteilung unmittelbar augenscheinlich. Da die Kolumnen wie der Graph eines Diagramms je nach Wort verschieden stark ausschlagen, wird dabei zugleich die Wortlänge 'vermessen'. Aus den unzähligen Wiederholungen ergeben sich zudem immer wieder eingängige Pattern, die wie auf den "I"-Seiten die Semantik der Schriftzeichen völlig in den Hintergrund rücken können.

Durch die Anordnung wird die strenge Sonettform mit ihren Endreimen in eine vertikale Struktur überführt, die in ihren alliterierenden Klangfolgen an Sound Poetry und dadaistischen Nonsense à la "Du deiner dich dir" (Kurt Schwitters' Anna Blume) erinnert. Dennoch wird man selbst in diesen Wortfolgen nicht selten auf überraschend Sinnfälliges stoßen. Gesteigert wird dieses wohl unaufhebbare Potential des Sprachmaterials zur Sinngenerierung bzw. unser wohl kaum unterdrückbarer Drang nach Sinnfindung durch die verschiedenen Leserichtungen: Denn selbstredend kann man den Index sowohl spaltenweise lesen (dabei ergibt sich z.B. "annoy anon anon another") als auch zeilenweise und sogar seitenübergreifend (z.B. "Eve's eye eyes face" und "tongues translate true truth ugly").

Ungeachtet solcher Funde ermuntert die – sowohl in semantischer als auch in klanglicher und visueller Hinsicht vollzogene – Auflösung der Sonette den Leser dazu, von der häufig betriebenen Konstruktion eines den Sonettzyklus zusammenhaltenden (biographistischen) Narrativs abzulassen und sich in dem seriell angeordneten Wortmaterial auf die mikroskopische Suche nach den subtilen – klanglichen, graphischen und

Regardless of these findings, the complete dissolution of the sonnets absolves the reader from relying on their biographically-driven narrative construction. Instead, with the serial ordering of the words he can go on a microscopic search for the poetic, graphic and semantic subtleties. This is so relevant for Shakespeare's cycle: "By frustrating our desire for story, Shakespeare teaches his readers – especially later readers – how to read in a new way."[1] It may be said that in Mark Rutkoski's *Words of Love*, the act of varying repetition compels a new, updated form of reading that is sensitized to the poetic qualities of the words themselves.

Annette Gilbert
translated by Vivien Knussi
New York, 2012

---

1. James Schiffer: "The Incomplete Narrative of the Sonnets," in: *A Companion to Shakespeare's Sonnets*, ed. by Michael Schoenfeldt, 2010, 45-56, 52.

semantischen – Differenzen zu begeben. Galt schon für Shakespeares Zyklus: "By frustrating our desire for story, Shakespeare teaches his readers – especially later readers – how to read in a new way"[1], so kann man auch für Mark Rutkoskis *Words of Love* verbuchen, dass sie in ihrem Akt der differierenden Wiederholung zu einer neuen, einer aktualisierenden und für die wortpoetischen Qualitäten sensibilisierenden Form der Lektüre zwingen.

Annette Gilbert
Berlin, 2012

---

1. James Schiffer: "The Incomplete Narrative of the Sonnets," in: *A Companion to Shakespeare's Sonnets*, ed. by Michael Schoenfeldt, 2010, 45-56, 52.

# WORDS OF LOVE

an index
of the words and their frequency
in the complete sonnets of
William Shakespeare

*Worn out phrases and longing gazes*
*Won't get you where you want to go....*

from "Words of Love" by The Mamas and the Papas,
lyrics by John Phillips

a
a
a
a
a
a
a
a
a
a
a
a
a
a
a
a
a
a
a
a
a
a
a
a
a
a
a
a
a
a
a
a
a
a
a
a
a
a
a
a
a
a
a
a
a
a
a
a
a
a
a
a
a
a
a
a
a
a
a
a
a
a
a
a
a
a
a
a
a
a
a
a
a
a
a
a
a
a
a
a
a
a
a
a
a
a
a
a
a
a
a
a
a
a
a
a
a
a
a
a
a
a
a
a
a
a
a
a
a
a
a
a
a
a
a
a
a
a
a
a
a
a
a
a
a
a
a
a
a
a
a
a
a
a
a
a
a
a
a
a
a
a
a
a
a
a
a
a
a
a
a
a
a

a
a
a
a
a
a
a
a
a
a
abhor
abhor
abide
abide
able
about
above
above
above
above
absence
absence
absence
absence
absence
absent
absent
absent
abundance
abundance
abundance
abundance
abundant
abus'd
abuse
abuse
abuse
abuses
abysm
accents
acceptable
acceptance
accessary
accident
accidents
account
account
account
account
accumulate
accuse
accuse
accusing
achieve
acknowledge
acquaintance
acquaintance
acquaintance
acquainted
acquainted
act
action
action
action
active
actor
add
add
add
add
added
added
adder's
addeth
adding
addition
addition
adieu
adjunct
adjunct
admire
admired
admiring
admit
admitted
Adonis
adore
a-doting
adulterate
advance
advantage
advantage
advantage
adverse
advis'd
advocate
afar
affable
affairs
affairs
affections
afford
affords
affords
afloat
afresh
after
after
after
after
after
after
after
after
after
after
after-loss
afterwards
again
again
again
again
again
again
again
again
again
again
against
against
against
against
against
against
against
against
against
against
against
against
against
against
against
against
against
against
age
age
age
age
age
age
age

age
age
age
age
age
age
age
age
age's
age's
ages
aggravate
ah
ah
ah
ah
ah
ah
ah
ah
aid
aid
air
air
air
air
alack
alack
alack
alas
alas
alchymy
alchymy
alien
alike
alive
alive
all
all
all
all
all
all
all
all
all
all
all
all
all
all
all
all
all
all
all
all
all
all
all
all
all
all
all
all
all
all
all
all
all
all
all
all
all
all
all
all
all
all
all
all
all
all
all
all
all
all
all
all
all
all
all
all
all
all
all
all
all
all
all
all
all
all
all
all
all
all
all
all
all
all
all
all
all
all
all
all
all
all
all
all
all
all
all
all
all
all
all
all
all
all
all
all
all
all
all
all
all
all
all
all
all
allay'd

| | | |
|---|---|---|
| all-eating | am | an |
| allege | am | an |
| all-oblivious | am | an |
| allow | am | an |
| allow | am | an |
| all-the-world | am | an |
| all-too-near | am | an |
| all-too-precious | am | an |
| almost | am | anchor'd |
| almost | am | and |
| almost | am | and |
| aloft | am | and |
| alone | am | and |
| alone | am | and |
| alone | am | and |
| alone | am | and |
| alone | am | and |
| alone | am | and |
| alone | am | and |
| alone | am | and |
| alone | am | and |
| alone | am | and |
| alone | am | and |
| alone | am | and |
| alone | am | and |
| alone | am | and |
| alone | am | and |
| alone | am | and |
| alone | am | and |
| alone | am | and |
| alone | am | and |
| already | am | and |
| alter | am | and |
| alteration | amazeth | and |
| alter'd | ambush | and |
| alter'd | Amen | and |
| altering | amends | and |
| alters | amiss | and |
| alters | amiss | and |
| although | amiss | and |
| although | among | and |
| although | among | and |
| although | among | and |
| although | an | and |
| although | an | and |
| although | an | and |
| although | an | and |
| although | an | and |
| always | an | and |
| am | an | and |
| am | an | and |

and and and
and and and
and and and
and and and
and and and
and and and
and and and
and and and
and and and
and and and
and and and
and and and
and and and
and and and
and and and
and and and
and and and
and and and
and and and
and and and
and and and
and and and
and and and
and and and
and and and
and and and
and and and
and and and
and and and
and and and
and and and
and and and
and and and
and and and
and and and
and and and
and and and
and and and
and and and
and and and
and and and
and and and
and and and
and and and
and and and
and and and
and and and
and and and
and and and
and and and
and and and

and
and
and
and
and
and
and
and
and
and
and
and
and
and
and
and
and
and
and
and
and
and
and
and
and
and
and
and
and
and
and
and
and
and
and
and
and
and
and
and
and
and
and
and
and
and
and
and
and
and
and
and
and
and
and
and
and
and
and
and
and
and
and
and
and
and
and
and
and
and
and
and
and
and
and
and
and
and
and
and
and
and
and
and
and
and
and
and
and
and
and
and
and
and
and
and
and
and
and
and
and
and
and
and
and
and
and
and
and
and
and
and
and
and
and
and
and
and
and
and
and
and
and
and
and
and
and
and
and
and
and
and
and
and
and
and
and
and
and
and
and
and
and
and
and
and
and
and
and
and
and
and
and

and
and
and
and
and
and
and
and
and
and
and
and
and
and
and
and
and
and
and
and
and
and
and
and
and
and
and
and
and
and
and
and
and
and
and
and
and
and
and
and
and
and
and
and
and
and
and
and
and
and
and

and
and
and
and
and
and
and
and
and
and
and
and
and
and
and
and
and
and
and
and
and
and
and
and
and
and
and
and
and
and
and
and
and
and
and
and
and
and
and
and
and
and
and
and
and
and
and
and
and
and
and

and
and
and
and
and
and
and
and
and
and
and
and
and
and
and
and
and
and
and
and
and
and
and
and
and
and
and
and
and
and
and
and
and
and
and
and
and
and
and
anew
anew
anew
angel
angel
angel
angel
angel
anger
angry
annex'd
annoy

| | | |
|---|---|---|
| anon | apple | are |
| anon | applying | are |
| another | approve | are |
| another | approve | are |
| another | approve | are |
| another | April | are |
| another | April | are |
| another | April | are |
| another | April's | are |
| another | are | are |
| another | are | are |
| another | are | are |
| another's | are | are |
| another's | are | are |
| another's | are | are |
| answer | are | are |
| answer | are | are |
| answer | are | are |
| answer'd | are | are |
| answers | are | are |
| anticipate | are | are |
| antique | are | are |
| antique | are | are |
| antique | are | are |
| antique | are | are |
| antique | are | are |
| antiquity | are | are |
| antiquity | are | are |
| any | are | argument |
| any | are | argument |
| any | are | argument |
| any | are | argument |
| any | are | argument |
| any | are | argument |
| any | are | aright |
| any | are | arise |
| any | are | arising |
| any | are | array |
| anything | are | arrest |
| apparel | are | Art |
| appeal | are | art |
| appear | are | art |
| appear | are | art |
| appear | are | art |
| appear | are | art |
| appearance | are | art |
| appears | are | art |
| appetite | are | art |
| appetite | are | art |
| appetite | are | art |
| appetites | are | art |

art
art
art
art
art
art
art
art
art
art
art
art
art
art
art
art
art
art
art
art
art
art
art
art
art
art
art
art
art
art
art
art
art
art
art
art
art
art
art's
arts
as
as
as
as
as
as
as
as
as
as
as

as
as
as
as
as
as
as
as
as
as
as
as
as
as
as
as
as
as
as
as
as
as
as
as
as
as
as
as
as
as
as
as
as
as
as
as
as
as
as
as
as
as
as
as
as
as
as
as
as
as
as

as
as
as
as
as
as
as
as
as
as
as
as
as
as
as
as
as
as
as
as
as
as
as
as
as
as
as
as
as
as
as
as
as
as
as
as
as
as
as
as
as
as
as
as
as
as
as
as
as
as
as

as
as
as
as
as
as
as
ashes
aside
aside
askance
ask'd
asleep
asleep
aspect
assail'd
assail'd
assemble
assistance
assur'd
assur'd
assure
assured
assured
astonished
astronomy
at
at
at
at
at
at
at
at
at
at
at
at
at
at
at
at
at
at
at
at
at
at
at
at
at

at
attaint
attainted
attend
attending
attending
audit
audit
audit
aught
aught
augurs
authorising
authority
autumn
autumn
awake
awakes
awards
away
away
away
away
away
away
away
away
away
away
away
away
away
away
away
away
away
away
ay
aye

babe
babe
babe
babe
back
back
back
back
back
back
back

back
back
backward
bad
bad
bad
bad
bad
bad
bad
badges
badness
bail
bail
bait
balmy
bankrupt
banks
banquet
bar
bare
bare
bare
bare
bareness
bareness
bark
bark
barren
barren
barren
barren
barren
barrenly
bars
bars
base
base
base
base
base
bases
basest
basest
basest
bastard
bastard
bastard
bath
bath
bath

bath
battering
bay
be
be
be
be
be
be
be
be
be
be
be
be
be
be
be
be
be
be
be
be
be
be
be
be
be
be
be
be
be
be
be
be
be
be
be
be
be
be
be
be
be
be
be
be
be
be
be
be
be
be
be
be
be
be
be
be
be
be
be
be
be
be
be
be
be
be
be
be
be
be
be
be
be
be
be
be
be
be
be
be
be
be
be
be
be
be
be
be
be
be
be
be
be
be
be
be
be
be
be
be
be
be
be
be
be
be
be
be
be
be
be
be
be
be
be
be
be
be
be
be
be
be
be
be
be
be
be
be
be
be
be
be
be
be
be
be
be
be
be
be
be
be
be
be
be
be
be
be
be
beams
bear
bear
bear
bear
bear
bear
bear
bear

bear
bear
bear
bear
beard
bearer
bearing
bearing
bearing
bears
bears
bears
bear'st
beast
beast
beated
beauteous
beauteous
beauteous
beauteous
beauteous
beauteous
beauteous
beauteous
beauteous
beauties
beauties
beauties
beauties
beautiful
beauty
beauty
beauty
beauty
beauty
beauty
beauty
beauty
beauty
beauty
beauty
beauty
beauty
beauty
beauty
beauty
beauty
beauty
beauty
beauty
beauty

beauty
beauty
beauty
beauty
beauty
beauty
beauty
beauty
beauty
beauty
beauty
beauty
beauty
beauty
beauty
beauty
beauty
beauty
beauty
beauty
beauty
beauty
beauty
beauty
beauty
beauty
beauty
beauty
beauty
beauty
beauty
beauty's
beauty's
beauty's
beauty's
beauty's
beauty's
beauty's
beauty's
beauty's
beauty's
beauty's
beauty's
beauty's
beauty's
beauty's
beauty's
beauty's
beauty's
because
because

because
beck
become
becomes
becomes
becoming
becoming
bed
beds'
bed-vow
been
been
been
been
been
been
befits
before
before
before
before
before
before
before
before
before
before
before
before
before
before
before
before
befriends
beggar
beggar'd
begin
begins
beguil'd
beguile
behaviour
behind
behind
behind
behind
behold
behold
behold
behold
behold
behold
behold

being
being
being
being
being
being
being
being
being
being
being
being
being
being
being
being
being
being
being
being
being
being
being
being
being
being
being
being
being
being
being
being
belied
belied
believe
believe
believe
believe
believed
bell
belong
belong
belongs
belongs
belov'd
belov'd
belov'd
beloved
bending
bending
bends
benefit
benefit
bent
bent
bequest
bereft
beseechers
beseem
beshrew
beside
besides
besides
besiege
besiege
besmear'd
best
best
best
best
best
best
best
best
best
best
best
best
best
best
best
best
best
best
best
best
best
best
best
bestow
bestow'st
betray
betray
betraying
better
better
better
better
better
better
better
better
better
better
better
better
better
better
better
better
better
better
better
better'd
bettering
betwixt
bevel
bewailed
beweep
beyond
bid
bide
'bide
bids
bier
big
bind
bird
birds
birds
birds
birth
birth
birth
birth
birth
bitter
bitter
bitterness
bitterness
black
black
black
black
black
black
black
black
black
black
black
black
black

blam'd
blam'd
blame
blame
blame
blame
blanks
blazon
blenches
bless'd
blessed
blessed
blessed
blessed
blessed
blessed
blessed
blessed-fair
blesses
blessing
blessings
blest
blind
blind
blind
blind
blind
blind
blindness
bliss
blood
blood
blood
blood
blood
blood
blood
blood
bloody
bloody
bloody
blot
blot
blot
blots
blow
blunt
blunt
blunt
blunter
blunting
blush
blushing
blushing
boast
boast
boast
boast
boast
boat
body
body
body
body
body's
body's
body's
body's
bold
bold
boldness
bond
bonds
bonds
bonds
bones
book
book
book
book
book
book
books
boot
bootless
bore
bore
born
born
born
born
born
born
born
borne
borne
borrow'd
borrow'd
bosom
bosom
bosom's
bosom's
bosoms
both
both
both
both
both
both
both
both
both
both
both
both
both
both
both
both
both
bough
boughs
bound
bound
boundless
bounteous
bounteous
bounty
bounty
bow
bow
boy
boy
boy
brag
brain
brain
brain
brain
brain
brains
brand
brand
brand
brand
brand
brass
brass
brass
brass
brave
brave
brave

bravery
breach
break
break
break
break
breast
breast
breast
breast
breast
breast
breast
breasts
breath
breath
breath
breath
breath
breath
breath
breath'd
breathe
breathe
breathers
breathes
bred
bred
breed
breed
breeds
brief
brief
brief
bright
bright
bright
bright
bright
bright
bright
bright
bright
bright
bright
brightness
bring
bring
bring
bring
bring
bring
bring
bring
brings
brings
bristly
broad
broils
broke
broke
broken
brood
brought
brought
brought
brow
brow
brow
brow
brow
brow
brow
brow
bud
bud
budding
buds
buds
buds
buds
builded
building
built
built
burden
buried
buried
buried
buried
buried
buriest
burn
burn
burn
burn'd
burning
burthen
burthen
burthens
busy
but
but
but
but
but
but
but
but
but
but
but
but
but
but
but
but
but
but
but
but
but
but
but
but
but
but
but
but
but
but
but
but
but
but
but
but
but
but
but
but
but
but
but
but
but
but
but
but
but
but
but
but
but

but
but
but
but
but
but
but
but
but
but
but
but
but
but
but
but
but
but
but
but
but
but
but
but
but
but
but
but
but
but
but
but
but
but
but
but
but
but
but
but
but
but
but
but
but
but
but
but
but
but
but
but
but
but
but
but
but
but
but
but
but
but
but
but
but
but
but
but
but
but
but
but
but
but
but
but
but
but
but
but
but
but
but
but
but
but
but
but
but
but
but
but
but
but
but
but
but
but
but
but
but
but
but
but
but
but
but
but
but
but
but
buy
by
by
by
by
by
by
by
by
by
by
by
by
by
by
by
by
by
by
by
by
by
by
by
by
by
by
by
by
by
by
by
by
by
by
by
by
by
by
by
by
by

| | | |
|---|---|---|
| by | by | can |
| by | by | can |
| by | by | can |
| by | | can |
| by | call | can |
| by | call | can |
| by | call | can |
| by | call | can |
| by | call | can |
| by | call | can |
| by | call | can |
| by | call | can |
| by | call | can |
| by | call | can |
| by | call'd | can |
| by | call'd | can |
| by | calls | can |
| by | calls | cancell'd |
| by | calls | candles |
| by | calls | canker |
| by | calls | canker |
| by | came | canker |
| by | came | canker |
| by | came | canker-blooms |
| by | can | cannot |
| by | can | cannot |
| by | can | cannot |
| by | can | cannot |
| by | can | cannot |
| by | can | cannot |
| by | can | cannot |
| by | can | cannot |
| by | can | cannot |
| by | can | cannot |
| by | can | canopy |
| by | can | canopy |
| by | can | canst |
| by | can | canst |
| by | can | canst |
| by | can | canst |
| by | can | canst |
| by | can | canst |
| by | can | canst |
| by | can | captain |
| by | can | captain |
| by | can | captive |
| by | can | car |
| by | can | carcanet |
| by | can | care |
| by | can | care |
| by | can | care |

care
care
care
careful
careful
carry
carv'd
carve
case
cast
cast
catch
catch
catch
catch
cause
cause
cause
cease
celestial
censures
centre
ceremony
certain
chance
change
change
change
change
change
change
change
change
change
change
change
change
changes
changing
changing
character
character
character
character'd
charg'd
charge
charter
charter
chary
chase
chase
chaste
cheap
cheater
check
check
check'd
check'd
cheek
cheek
cheek
cheek
cheek
cheeks
cheeks
cheeks
cheeks
cheer
cheered
cherish
cherubins
chest
chest
chest
chide
chide
chide
chide
chide
chiding
chief
chief
child
child
child
child
child
child
child
child
children
children's
chips
choirs
choose
chopp'd
chose
chronicle
churl
churl
churls
'cide
civil
clay
clean
clear
clear
clear
clearer
clearer
clears
clerk
climb'd
cloak
clock
clock
closet
closure
cloud
cloud
clouds
clouds
clouds
clouds
cold
cold
cold
cold
cold
cold
cold
colour
colour
colour
colour'd
come
come
come
come
come
come
come
come
come
come
come
come
come
come
come
comes
comes
comfort

comfort
comfort
comfort
coming
coming
commanded
commence
commend
comment
comment
comments
comments
commit
commits
commits
committed
common
common
common
common
compar'd
compare
compare
compare
compare
compare
compare
compass
compeers
compil'd
compile
complain
complexion
complexion
complexion
composed
composition
compound
compounded
compounds
compounds
conceal'd
conceit
conceit
conceit
concord
concord
condemned
confess
confess'd
confin'd
confin'd
confin'd
confine
confound
confound
confounded
confounding
confounds
confounds
confounds
conquer'd
conquest
conquest
conquest
conscience
conscience
conscience
consecrate
consent
consider
conspire
constancy
constancy
constancy
constant
constant
constant
consum'd
consum'st
contain
contains
contend
content
content
contented
contented
contented
contents
continual
contracted
contracted-new
contrary
control
control
control
controlling
controlling
convert
converted
converted
convertest
cool
cools
copy
copy
coral
correct
correction
correspondence
corrupt
corrupt
corrupting
cost
cost
cost
costly
could
could
could
could
could
could
could
could
could
could
couldst
count
count
count
count
counted
countenance
counterfeit
counterfeit
counterpart
counting
counting
couplement
course
course
course
courses
cover
cover
cover
covetous
coward
crave
crawls
created
created

creating
creation
creation
creature
creatures
creatures
credit
creep
crests
cries
cries
crime
crime
crime
crime
critic
crooked
crooked
cross
cross
cross
cross'd
crow
crow
crown
crown'd
crown'd
crown'd
crowned
crowning
cruel
cruel
cruel
cruel
cruel
cruel
cruel
cruel
crush'd
cry
cry
crying
crystal
cunning
cunning
cunning
cup
Cupid
Cupid
cure
cure
cure
cure
cure
cured
cures
curious
curls
curse
curse
cut

daily
daily
daily
damask'd
dancing
dare
dare
dare
dare
dark
dark
dark
darkening
darkly
darkness
darling
dart
date
date
date
date
date
dateless
dateless
dates
day
day
day
day
day
day
day
day
day
day
day
day
day
day
day
day
day
day
day
day
day
day
day
day
day
day's
days
days
days
days
days
days
days
days
days
days
days
days
days
days
days
days
days
dead
dead
dead
dead
dead
dead
dead
dead
dead
dead
dead
dead
dead
dead
dead
dead
deaf
dear
dear
dear
dear
dear
dear

dear
dear
dear
dear
dear
dear
dear
dear
dear
dear
dear
dear
dear
dear
dear
dearer
dearer
dearest
dearest
dearest
dearly
dear-purchas'd
dearth
dearths
Death
Death
Death
Death
Death
Death
death
death
death
death
death
death
death
death
death
death-bed
Death's
Death's
death's
death's
deaths
deaths
debarr'd
debate
debateth
debt
debtor
decay
decay
decay
decay
decay
decay
decay
decay
decay
decay'd
decays
decease
decease
deceased
deceased
deceiv'd
deceive
deceive
deceived
deceivest
December's
declines
decrease
decrease
decree
decrees
decrepit
dedicated
deeds
deeds
deeds
deeds
deeds
deeds
deeds
deeds
deeds
deeds
deem
deem'd
deem'd
deep
deep
deep
deep
deep
deep
deep
deep
deepest
defac'd
deface
defeat
defeated
defect
defect
defects
defence
defence
defence
defendant
define
deformed'st
defy
delay'd
delight
delight
delight
delight
delight
delight
delight
delight
delighted
delights
delights
deliver'd
delivers
delves
denied
denote
deny
deny
depart
depart
departest
depend
depends
depends
derive
describe
descriptions
desert
desert
desert
deserts
deserts
deserv'd
deserve
deserves
deserving
deserv'st

| | | |
|---|---|---|
| desir'd | did | discloses |
| desire | did | discontent |
| desire | did | discontent |
| desire | did | discourse |
| desire | did | disdain |
| desire | did | disdain |
| desire | did | disdaineth |
| desire | did | disdains |
| desire | did | diseas'd |
| desire | did | diseas'd |
| desire | did | disease |
| desire | did | disgrac'd |
| desired | did | disgrace |
| desiring | did | disgrace |
| despair | did | disgrace |
| despair | did | disgrace |
| despair | did | disgrace |
| despatch | did | disgrace |
| desperate | did | disgrace |
| despis'd | did | disgrace |
| despise | did | dispense |
| despise | didst | disperse |
| despised | didst | dispos'd |
| despised | didst | dispraise |
| despising | die | dissuade |
| despite | die | distance |
| despite | die | distemper'd |
| despite | die | distillation |
| despite | die | distill'd |
| despite | die | distill'd |
| despite | die | distill'd |
| destroys | die | distils |
| detain | die | distraction |
| determinate | die | divert |
| determination | die | divide |
| determined | die | divided |
| devil | died | divine |
| devis'd | died | divine |
| devise | dies | divining |
| devise | diest | do |
| devour | difference | do |
| devouring | different | do |
| dial | dig | do |
| dial-hand | dignified | do |
| dial's | dignifies | do |
| Dian's | dignity | do |
| did | dimm'd | do |
| did | directed | do |
| did | directly | do |
| did | disabled | do |
| did | disarm'd | do |

| | | |
|---|---|---|
| do | do | dost |
| do | do | dost |
| do | do | dost |
| do | do | dost |
| do | do | dost |
| do | do | dost |
| do | do | dost |
| do | do | dost |
| do | do | dost |
| do | do | dost |
| do | do | dost |
| do | do | dost |
| do | do | dost |
| do | do | dost |
| do | do | dote |
| do | do | dote |
| do | do | doth |
| do | do | doth |
| do | do | doth |
| do | do | doth |
| do | do | doth |
| do | do | doth |
| do | doctor-like | doth |
| do | doing | doth |
| do | doing | doth |
| do | done | doth |
| do | done | doth |
| do | done | doth |
| do | done | doth |
| do | done | doth |
| do | doom | doth |
| do | doom | doth |
| do | doom | doth |
| do | doom | doth |
| do | doom | doth |
| do | dost | doth |
| do | dost | doth |
| do | dost | doth |
| do | dost | doth |
| do | dost | doth |
| do | dost | doth |
| do | dost | doth |
| do | dost | doth |
| do | dost | doth |
| do | dost | doth |
| do | dost | doth |
| do | dost | doth |
| do | dost | doth |
| do | dost | doth |
| do | dost | doth |
| do | dost | doth |

doth
doth
doth
doth
doth
doth
doth
doth
doth
doth
doth
doth
doth
doth
doth
doth
doth
doth
doth
doth
doth
doth
doth
doth
doth
doth
doth
doth
doth
doth
doth
doth
doth
doth
doth
doth
doth
doth
doth
doth
doth
doth
doth
doth
doth
doth
doth
doth
doth
doth
doth

doting
double
double
double-vantage
doubt
doubting
doubting
dove
down
down
down
down
down-ras'd
drain'd
draw
draw
draw
drawn
drawn
drawn
dreading
dream
dream
dreaming
dreams
dreams
dregs
dress
dress'd
dressing
dressings
drink
drink
drinks
drooping
drop
drops
dross
drown
drowns
drudge
drugs
drunk
dry
due
due
due
due
due
due
dull

dull
dull
dull
dull
dull
dulling
dully
dulness
dumb
dumb
dumb
dumb
dumb
dumb
dun
durst
dust
dust
duteous
duty
duty
duty
dwell
dwell
dwell
dwell
dwell
dwell
dwellers
dwells
dy'd
dy'd
dye
dyer's
dying

each
each
each
each
each
each
each
each
each
each
each
each
each
each
each

eager
ear
ear
ear
early
ears
ears
earth
earth
earth
earth
earth
earth
earth
earth
earth
earth
earth
earthly
eas'd
ease
ease
east
easy
eat
eat
eat
eclipse
eclipses
eclipses
edge
edge
edge
e'er
effect
effect
effect
effectually
either
either
either's
either's
elder
elements
elements
eloquence
else
else
else
else
else
elsewhere
elsewhere
elsewhere
embassage
embassy
enclose
end
end
end
end
end
end
end
end
end
end
endeared
ending
endless
endow'd
endur'd
endure
enemies
enemies
enfeebled
enforc'd
engraft
engrafted
engross'd
enjoy
enjoy'd
enjoyer
enjoys
enlarg'd
enlighten
enmity
enough
enough
enough
enough
enough
enough
enrich
ensconce
entertain
entitled
entombed
envy
envy
epitaph
equal
equipage
ere
ere
ere
ere
ere
ere
err
err'd
error
errors
errors
errors
errors
erst
essays
esteem
esteem
esteem'd
esteem'd
esteeming
estimate
eternal
eternal
eternal
eternal
eternal
eternal
eternity
eternity
eternity
even
even
even
even
even
even
even
even
even
even
even
even
even
even
even
even
even
even
even
even

even
even
even
even
ever
ever
ever
ever
ever
ever
ever
ever
ever
ever
ever
ever-fixed
evermore
evermore
evermore
every
every
every
every
every
every
every
every
every
every
every
every
every
every
every
every
every
every
every
every
every
every
every
every
every
everything
everywhere
everywhere
everywhere
everywhere
everywhere
Eve's
evident
evil
evil
evil
evil
example
exceed
exceeded
exceeds
excel
excellence
excellence
excellent
except
excess
exchang'd
exchequer
excuse
excuse
excuse
excuse
excuse
excuse
excuse
excusing
executor
expense
expense
expense
expiate
expir'd
expire
express
express
express'd
express'd
express'd
expressing
extant
extern
external
extreme
extreme
extremity
eye
eye
eye
eye
eye
eye
eye
eye
eye
eye
eye
eye
eye
eye
eye
eye
eye
eye
eye
eye
eye
eye
eye
eye
eye
eye
eye
eye
eye
eye
eye
eye
eye
eye
eye
eye
eye
eyed
eyelids
eyelids
eye's
eyes
eyes
eyes
eyes
eyes
eyes
eyes
eyes
eyes
eyes
eyes
eyes
eyes
eyes
eyes
eyes
eyes

| | | |
|---|---|---|
| eyes | face | fair |
| eyes | face | fair |
| eyes | face | fair |
| eyes | face | fair |
| eyes | face | fair |
| eyes | face | fair |
| eyes | face | fair |
| eyes | face | fair |
| eyes | faces | fair |
| eyes | faces | fair |
| eyes | faculty | fairer |
| eyes | fade | fairer |
| eyes | fade | fairer |
| eyes | fade | fairest |
| eyes | fadeth | fairest |
| eyes | fading | fairest |
| eyes | fading | fairest |
| eyes | faint | fairest |
| eyes | fair | fairing |
| eyes | fair | fairly |
| eyes | fair | faith |
| eyes | fair | faith |
| eyes | fair | faith |
| eyes | fair | faith |
| eyes | fair | faith |
| eyes | fair | fall |
| eyes | fair | fall |
| eyes | fair | fall |
| eyes | fair | falls |
| eyes | fair | false |
| eyes | fair | false |
| eyes | fair | false |
| eyes | fair | false |
| eyes | fair | false |
| eyes | fair | false |
| eyes' | fair | false |
| eyes' | fair | false |
| eyes' | fair | false |
| eysell | fair | false |
| | fair | false |
| face | fair | false |
| face | fair | false |
| face | fair | false |
| face | fair | false |
| face | fair | false |
| face | fair | false |
| face | fair | false |
| face | fair | falsehood |
| face | fair | falsehood |
| face | fair | falsely |
| face | fair | false-speaking |

fame
fame
fame
familiar
famine
famish'd
famoused
far
far
far
far
far
far
far
far
far
far
far
far
far
far
far
far
farewell
faring
farther
farther
farther
farther
farthest
farthest
fashion
fashion
fast
fast
fast
fast
fast
faster
fate
father
father
fault
fault
fault
faults
faults
faults
faults
faults
faults
faults
faults
favour
favour
favour
favourites
fawn
fear
fear
fear
fear
fear
fear
fear
fear
fearful
fearfully
fearing
fears
fears
fears
fears
fears
fears
feast
feast
feasting
feasts
feather'd
feathers
featur'd
feature
featureless
fed
fee
feeble
feed
feeding
feeding
feeding
feeds
feeds
feed'st
feel
feel
feeling
feeling
feel'st
fell
fell
fell
fell
fell
felt
female
fester
fever
fever
few
fickle
field
fiend
fiend
fierce
fierce
fiery
fight
fight
fight
figur'd
figure
figures
filching
fil'd
fill
fill
fill
fill'd
fill'd
fill'd
find
find
find
find
find
find
find
find
find
find
find
find
find
find
find
find
finding
finding
finds
finds
fine
fine

| | | |
|---|---|---|
| finger | flesh | for |
| fingers | flesh | for |
| fingers | flesh | for |
| fingers | flies | for |
| fire | flies | for |
| fire | flies | for |
| fire | flourish | for |
| fire | flow | for |
| fire | flower | for |
| fire | flower | for |
| fire | flower | for |
| fire | flower | for |
| fire | flower | for |
| fire | flowers | for |
| firm | flowers | for |
| first | flowers | for |
| first | flowers | for |
| first | flowers | for |
| first | flowers | for |
| first | flowers | for |
| first | flowers | for |
| first | flown | for |
| first | fly | for |
| first | foe | for |
| first | foes | for |
| first | foes | for |
| first | foes | for |
| first-born | foil'd | for |
| fit | foison | for |
| fitted | foist | for |
| five | follow | for |
| five | follow | for |
| five | follow'd | for |
| fix'd | follows | for |
| fix'd | folly | for |
| flame | folly | for |
| flame | fond | for |
| flame | fond | for |
| flatter | food | for |
| flatter | fool | for |
| flatter | fool | for |
| flatter'd | fool | for |
| flatterer | fool'd | for |
| flattery | foolish | for |
| flattery | fools | for |
| flattery | foot | for |
| fled | foot | for |
| fled | foot | for |
| fleece | for | for |
| fleeting | for | for |
| fleets | for | for |

for
for
for
for
for
for
for
for
for
for
for
for
for
for
for
for
for
for
for
for
for
for
for
for
for
for
for
for
for
for
for
for
for
for
for
for
for
for
for
for
for
for
for
for
for
for
for
for
for
for
for

for
for
for
for
for
for
for
for
for
for
for
for
for
for
for
for
for
for
for
for
for
for
for
for
for
for
for
for
for
for
for
for
for
for
for
for
for
for
for
for
for
for
for
for
for
for
for
for
for
for
for

for
for
for
for
for
for
for
for
for
for
for
for
for
for
for
for
for
forbear
forbear
forbid
forbid
forbid
forbidden
forc'd
force
force
'fore
fore-bemoaned
foregoing
foregone
forests
forfeit
forfeit
forged
forget
forget
forgetful
forgetfulness
forgett'st
forgive
forgot
forgot
forgot
forgot
forgotten
forlorn
form
form
form
form
form

| | | |
|---|---|---|
| form | found | from |
| form | found | from |
| form | found | from |
| form | fountains | from |
| form | four | from |
| form | fragrant | from |
| former | frailer | from |
| former | frailties | from |
| former | frailties | from |
| former | frame | from |
| forsake | frame | from |
| forsake | frame | from |
| forsaken | frame | from |
| forsworn | frank | from |
| forsworn | frantic | from |
| forsworn | free | from |
| forsworn | free | from |
| forth | free | from |
| forth | free | from |
| forth | freedom | from |
| forth | freezings | from |
| forth | frequent | from |
| forth | fresh | from |
| forth | fresh | from |
| fortify | fresh | from |
| fortify | fresh | from |
| Fortune | fresh | from |
| fortune | fresh | from |
| fortune | fresh | from |
| fortune | fresher | from |
| fortune | friend | from |
| fortune | friend | from |
| Fortune's | friend | from |
| fortune's | friend | from |
| fortune's | friend | from |
| forty | friend | from |
| forward | friend | from |
| forwards | friend | from |
| foul | friend | from |
| foul | friend | from |
| foul | friend | from |
| foul | friend | from |
| foul | friend | from |
| foul | friend | from |
| foul | friend's | from |
| found | friend's | from |
| found | friends | from |
| found | friends | from |
| found | friends | from |
| found | from | from |
| found | from | from |

from
from
from
from
from
from
from
from
from
from
from
from
from
from
from
from
from
from
from
from
from
from
from
from
from
from
from
from
front
frost
frown
frown
frown
frowns
frown'st
fruit
fuel
fulfil
fulfil
full
full
full
full
full
full
full
full
full
full
full
full

full
fulness
function
furrows
fury

gain
gain
gain
gain
gainer
gains
'gainst
'gainst
'gainst
'gainst
'gainst
'gainst
gait
gaol
gardens
garments
garments'
gate
gates
gather'd
gaudy
gave
gave
gave
gave
gave
gav'st
gav'st
gav'st
gay
gay
gaz'd
gaze
gaze
gazers
gazeth
gazing
gems
general
general
general
gentle
gentle
gentle
gentle

gentle
gentle
gentle
gentle
gentle
gentle
gentle
gentle
gentle
gentle
gentlest
gently
get
ghastly
ghost
gift
gift
gift
gift
gift
gifts
gilded
gilded
gilded
gilding
gilding
gild'st
girded
give
give
give
give
give
give
give
give
give
give
give
give
give
give
give
give
give
give
give
give
give
give
give

give
give
give
give
given
given
given
given
gives
gives
gives
gives
gives
gives
gives
gives
giving
giving
glad
glad
gladly
glance
glance
glass
glass
glass
glass
glass
glass
glass
glass
glass
glass
glazed
glorious
glory
glory
glory
glory
glory
glory
glory
glory
glowing
glutton
gluttoning
go
go
go
go
go
go
God
god
goddess
goddess
goes
goest
going
gold
gold
golden
golden
golden
golden
golden
gone
gone
gone
gone
gone
gone
gone
gone
gone
good
good
good
good
good
good
good
good
good
good
good
good
good
good
good
goodly
goodness
goodness
gor'd
got
got
got
governs
grace
grace
grace
grace
grace
grace
grace
grace
grace
grace
grace
graced
graces
graces
graces
graces
graces
gracious
gracious
gracious
gracious
gracious
graciously
grant
grant
grant
grant
granting
grave
grave
grave
graven
graves
gravity
great
great
great
great
great
great
great
great
great
great
greater
greater
greater
greatest
Grecian
'greeing
green
green
green
green
green

greet
greet
greet
grew
grew
grew
grew
grew
grey
grief
grief
grief
grief
grief
grief's
griefs
grievances
griev'd
grieve
grind
groan
groan
groan
groan
groans
gross
gross
grossly
ground
ground
ground
grounded
grounded
grow
grow
grow
grow
grow
grow
grow
grow
growest
growing
growing
growing
grown
grown
grown
grown
grows
grows

grows
grows
grow'st
grow'st
growth
growth
growth
guard
guard
guess
guess
guest
guest
guides
guilt
guilty
guilty
gulls
gust
gusts

habit
habitation
had
had
had
had
had
had
had
had
had
had
had
had
had
had
had
had
hadst
hadst
hair
hairs
half
half
half
hallow'd
halt
hammer'd
hand
hand

hand
hand
hand
hand
hand
hand
hand
hand
hand
hand
hand
hand
hand
hand
hand
hands
hands
hang
hang
hang
hanging
hap
haply
haply
haply
happier
happier
happier
happies
happy
happy
happy
happy
happy
happy
happy
happy
happy
happy
happy
hard
harder
hardest
harmful
harsh
harvest
hast
hast
hast
hast
hast

hast
hast
hast
hast
hast
hast
hast
hast
hast
hast
hast
hast
haste
haste
haste
hasten
hate
hate
hate
hate
hate
hate
hate
hate
hate
hate
hate
hate
hate
hate
hate
hate
hated
hate's
hateth
hath
hath
hath
hath
hath
hath
hath
hath
hath
hath
hath
hath
hath
hath
hath
hath

hath
hath
hath
hath
hath
hath
hath
hath
hath
hath
hath
hath
hath
hath
hath
hath
hath
hath
hath
hath
hath
hath
hath
hath
hath
hath
hath
hatred
have
have
have
have
have
have
have
have
have
have
have
have
have
have
have
have
have
have
have
have
have
have
have

have
have
have
have
have
have
have
have
have
have
have
have
have
have
have
have
have
have
have
have
have
have
have
have
have
have
have
have
have
have
have
have
have
have
have
have
have
have
have
have
have
have
have
have
have
have
have
have
have
have
have

have
have
have
having
having
having
having
having
having
hawks
hawks
he
he
he
he
he
he
he
he
he
he
he
he
he
he
he
he
he
he
he
he
he
he
he
he
he
he
he
he
he
he
he
he
he
he
he
he
he
he
he
he
he
he
he
head
head
head
head
head
head
heals
health
health
healthful
healthful
hear
hear
hear
hear
hear
hear
heard
hearing
hearsay
hear'st
heart
heart
heart
heart
heart
heart
heart
heart
heart
heart
heart
heart
heart
heart
heart
heart
heart
heart
heart
heart
heart
heart
heart
heart
heart
heart
heart
heart
heart
heart
heart
heart
heart
heart
heart
heart
heart
heart
heart
heart
heart
heart
heart
heart
heart
heart
heart
heart
heart
heart
heart-inflaming
heart's
heart's
heart's
heart's
heart's
heart's
heart's
hearts
hearts
hearts
hearts
heat
heat
heat
heat
heats
Heaven
Heaven
heaven
heaven
heaven
heaven
heaven
heaven
heaven
heaven
heaven
heaven

heaven
heavenly
heavenly
heavenly
Heaven's
heaven's
heaven's
heaven's
heaven's
heaven's
heavily
heavily
heavy
heavy
heavy
heavy
heavy
heavy
heed
height
height
height
heinous
heir
heir
heir
held
held
Helen's
hell
hell
hell
hell
hell
hell
hell
hell
help
help
help
help
hems
hence
hence
hence
hence
hence
hence
her
her
her

her
her
her
her
her
her
her
her
her
her
her
her
her
her
her
her
her
her
her
her
her
her
her
her
her
her
her
her
her
her
her
her
her
her
her
her
her
her
her
her
her
her
her
her
her
her
her
her
herald
herd
here

here
here
here
herein
here's
heretic
hers
herself
he's
hid
hid
hidden
hide
hide
hide
hide
hide
hideous
hideous
hides
hiding
hied
high
high
high
high
high-most
hill
him
him
him
him
him
him
him
him
him
him
him
him
him
him
him
him
him
him
him
him
him
him
him

him
him
him
him
him
him
him
him
him
him
him
him
him
him
him
himself
himself
hindmost
his
his
his
his
his
his
his
his
his
his
his
his
his
his
his
his
his
his
his
his
his
his
his
his
his
his
his
his
his
his
his
his
his

his
his
his
his
his
his
his
his
his
his
his
his
his
his
his
his
his
his
his
his
his
his
his
his
his
his
his
his
his
his
his
his
his
his
his
his
his
his
his
his
his
his
his
his
his
his
his
his
his
his
his

his
his
his
his
his
his
his
his
his
his
his
his
his
his
his
his
his
his
his
his
his
his
history
hits
hoisted
hold
hold
hold
hold
hold
hold
hold
hold
hold
hold
hold
hold
hold
holds
holds
holds
holds
holds
holy
holy
holy
holy
homage
home
home
home

honest
honey
honour
honour
honour
honour
honour
honour
honour
honouring
hooks
hope
hope
hope
hope
hope
hope
hopes
hopes
horse
horse
horses
hot
hot
hot
hounds
hour
hour
hour
hour
hour
hours
hours
hours
hours
hours
hours
hours
hours
hours
hours
hours
hours
house
housewife
how
how
how
how
how
how

how
how
how
how
how
how
how
how
how
how
how
how
how
how
how
how
how
how
how
how
how
how
how
how
how
how
how
how
how
how
how
how
how
how
hue
hue
hue
hue
hue
hues
huge
huge
hugely
humble
humble
humour
humour
hundred
hung
hung
hungry

hungry
hunted
hurt
husband
husband
husband
husbandry
husbandry
husband's
hush
hymn
hymns
hymns

I
I
I
I
I
I
I
I
I
I
I
I
I
I
I
I
I
I
I
I
I
I
I
I
I
I
I
I
I
I
I
I
I
I
I
I
I

I
I
I
I
I
I
I
I
I
I
I
I
I
I
I
I
I
I
I
I
I
I
I
I
I
I
I
I
I
I
I
I
I
I
I
I
I
I
I
I
I
I
I
I
I
I
I
I
I
I
I
I
I
I
I
I
I
I
I
I
I
I
I
I
I
I
I
I
I
I
I
I
I
I
I
I
I
I
I
I
I
I
I
I
I
I
I
I
I
I
I
I
I
I
I
I
I
I
I
I
I
I
I
I
I
I
I
I
I
I
I
I
I
I
I
I
I
I
I
I
I
I
I
I
I
I
I
I
I
I
I
I
I
I
I
I
I
I
I
I
I
I
I
I
I
I
I
I
I
I
I
I
I

I I I
I I I
I I I
I I I
I I I
I I I
I I I
I I I
I I I
I I I
I I I
I I I
I I I
I I I
I I I
I I I
I I I
I I I
I I I
I I I
I I I
I I I
I I I
I I I
I I I
I I I
I I I
I I I
I I I
I I I
I I I
I I I
I I I
I I I
I I I
I I I
I I I
I I I
I I I
I I I
I I I
I I I
I I I
I I I
I I I
I I I
I I I
I I I
I I I
I I I
I I I

I
idle
idle
idly
idol
idolatry
if
if
if
if
if
if
if
if
if
if
if
if
if
if
if
if
if
if
if
if
if
if
if
if
if
if
if
if
if
if
if
if
if
if
if
if
if
if
if
if
if
if
if
if
if

if
if
if
if
if
if
if
if
if
if
if
if
if
if
if
if
if
if
if
if
if
if
if
ignorance
ignorance
I'll
I'll
I'll
I'll
I'll
I'll
I'll
ill
ill
ill
ill
ill
ill
ill
ill
ill
ill
ill
ill
ill
ill
ill
ill
ill
ill
ills

ill-used
ill-wresting
image
image
image
image
images
imaginary
imitate
imitated
immortal
immured
impair
impanneled
impart
impeach'd
impediments
imperfect
impiety
import
importune
impregnable
impression
imprint
imprison'd
imprison'd
impute
in
in
in
in
in
in
in
in
in
in
in
in
in
in
in
in
in
in
in
in
in
in
in
in

in
in
in
in
in
in
in
in
in
in
in
in
in
in
in
in
in
in
in
in
in
in
in
in
in
in
in
in
in
in
in
in
in
in
in
in
in
in
in
in
in
in
in
in
in
in
in
in
in
in
in
in
in
in
in
in
in
in
in
in
in
in
in
in
in
in
in
in
in
in
in
in
in
in
in
in
in
in
in
in
in
in
in
in
in
in
in
in
in
in
in
in
in
in
in
in
in
in
in
in
in
in
in
in
in
in
in
in
in
in
in
in
in
in
in
in
in
in
in
in
in
in
in
in
in
in
in
in
in
in
in
in
in
in
in
in
in
in
in
in
in
in
in
in
in
in
in
in
in
in
in
in
in

in
in
in
in
in
in
in
in
in
in
in
in
in
in
in
in
in
in
in
in
in
in
in
in
in
in
in
in
in
in
in
in
in
in
in
in
in
in
in
in
in
in
in
in
in
in
in
in
in
in
in

in
in
in
in
in
in
in
in
in
in
in
in
in
in
in
in
in
in
in
in
in
in
in
in
in
in
in
in
in
in
in
in
in
in
in
in
in
in
in
in
in
in
in
in
in
in
in
in
in
in
in

in
in
in
in
in
in
in
in
in
in
in
in
in
in
in
in
in
in
in
in
in
in
in
in
in
in
in
in
in
in
in
in
in
in
in
in
in
in
in
in
in
in
in
in
incapable
incertainties
incertainty
inconstant
inconstant
increase
increase

| | | |
|---|---|---|
| increase | invention | is |
| increase | invited | is |
| increasing | inviting | is |
| indeed | invocate | is |
| indigest | invok'd | is |
| indirectly | inward | is |
| infant's | inward | is |
| infection | inward | is |
| infection | inward | is |
| infection | is | is |
| inferior | is | is |
| influence | is | is |
| influence | is | is |
| informer | is | is |
| inhabit | is | is |
| inhearse | is | is |
| inherit | is | is |
| inheritors | is | is |
| iniquity | is | is |
| injuries | is | is |
| injuries | is | is |
| injurious | is | is |
| injurious | is | is |
| injury | is | is |
| injury | is | is |
| injury | is | is |
| ink | is | is |
| ink | is | is |
| instant | is | is |
| instinct | is | is |
| insufficiency | is | is |
| insults | is | is |
| intelligence | is | is |
| intend | is | is |
| intents | is | is |
| interchange | is | is |
| interest | is | is |
| interest | is | is |
| interim | is | is |
| intermix'd | is | is |
| into | is | is |
| into | is | is |
| into | is | is |
| into | is | is |
| into | is | is |
| invent | is | is |
| invent | is | is |
| invention | is | is |
| invention | is | is |
| invention | is | is |
| invention | is | is |

| | | |
|---|---|---|
| is | is | it |
| is | is | it |
| is | is | it |
| is | is | it |
| is | is | it |
| is | is | it |
| is | is | it |
| is | is | it |
| is | is | it |
| is | is | it |
| is | is | it |
| is | is | it |
| is | is | it |
| is | is | it |
| is | is | it |
| is | is | it |
| is | is | it |
| is | is | it |
| is | is | it |
| is | is | it |
| is | is | it |
| is | is | it |
| is | is | it |
| is | is | it |
| is | issue | it |
| is | issue | it |
| is | issueless | it |
| is | is't | it |
| is | is't | it |
| is | it | it |
| is | it | it |
| is | it | it |
| is | it | it |
| is | it | it |
| is | it | it |
| is | it | it |
| is | it | it |
| is | it | it |
| is | it | it |
| is | it | it |
| is | it | it |
| is | it | it |
| is | it | it |
| is | it | it |
| is | it | it |
| is | it | it |
| is | it | it |
| is | it | it |
| is | it | it |
| is | it | it |
| is | it | it |

it
it
it
it
it
it
it
it
it
it
it
it
it
it
it
it
it
it
it
it
it
it
it
it
it
it
it
it
it
it
it
it
it
itself
itself
itself
itself
itself
itself
itself

jacks
jacks
jade
jaws
jealous
jealousy
jewel
jewel
jewel
jewel

jewels
jewels
join
jollity
journey
journey
joy
joy
joy
joy
joy
joy
joy
joy
judgment
judgment
judgment
judgment
judgment
judgment
judgment's
jump
Junes
just
just
just
just
justify

keen
keen
keep
keep
keep
keep
keep
keep
keep
keep
keep
keeps
keeps
keeps
keeps
keeps
keeps
keep'st
kept
kept
kept
key
kill

kill
kill
kill
kill
kills
kind
kind
kind
kind
kind
kind
kind
kind
kind
kind
kind
kind-hearted
kindness
kindness
kinds
king
king
kingdom
kingdoms
kingly
kings
kings'
kiss
kiss
kiss
kissing
knew
knew'st
knife
knife
knife
knife
knights
knit
know
know
know
know
know
know
know
know
know
know
know
know

know
know
know
know
know
knowing
knowing
knowing
knowing
knowledge
knowledge
knowledge
known
knows
knows
knows
knows
knows
knows
knows
knows
knows
knows
knows
know'st
know'st
know'st

labouring
lace
lack
lack
lack
lack
lack'd
lack'd
lacking
ladies
laid
laid
laid
lamb
lambs
lame
lame
lameness
land
languish'd
lap
large
large
large
large
large
largess
lark
lascivious
lascivious
last
last
lasting
latch
late
laugh'd
lawful
lawful
lawful
laws
lay
lay
lay
lays
lays
lays
lays
lead
lead
leads
leads
league
lean
leap
leap
leap'd
learn
learn
learn'd
learned's
learning
learning
lease
lease
lease
lease
leases
least
least
least
least
least
leave
leave
leave
leave
leave
leave
leave
leave
leave
leave
leave
leaves
leaves
leaves
leaves
leaves
leaves
leaves
leaves
leaving
leese
left
left
left
left
left
legacy
legions
leisure
leisure
leisure
leisure
lend
lend
lend
lend
lend
lends
lends
lends
lends
lengths
less
less
less
less
less
less
less
lesser
lesson
lest
lest
lest

lest
lest
lest
lest
lest
let
let
let
let
let
let
let
let
let
let
let
let
let
let
let
let
let
let
let
let
let
let
let
let
let
let
lets
level
level
liberty
liberty
lie
lie
lie
lie
lie
lie
lie
lie
lie
lie
lie
lie
lie
lies
lies
lies
lies
lies
lies
lies
lies
lies
lies
lies
lies
life
life
life
life
life
life
life
life
life
life
life
life
life
life
life
life
life
life
life
life
life
life
life
life's
lifts
light
light
light
light
light
light
light's
like
like
like
like
like
like
like
like
like
like
like
like
like
like
like
like
like
like
like
like
like
like
like
like
like
like
like
like
like
like
like
like
like
like
likeness
liker
lilies
lilies
lily
limbecs
limbs
limbs
limit
limits
limping
line
line
line
lines
lines
lines
lines
lines
lines
lines
lines
linger
lion's
lip
lips

lips
lips
lips
lips
lips
lips'
liquid
list
little
little
liv'd
liv'd
liv'd
liv'd
live
live
live
live
live
live
live
live
live
live
live
live
live
live
live
live
live
live
live
live
live
live
live
live
live
live
live
live
live
lively
lively
livery
lives
lives
lives
lives
lives
lives
lives
lives
lives
living
living
living
living
living
living
living
lo
lo
lo
loan
loathsome
lock'd
lodg'd
lofty
lofty
long
long
long
long
long
long
long
long
long
long
longer
longer
longer
longer
longer
longer
longing
long-liv'd
long-since
look
look
look
look
look
look
look
look
look
look
look
look
look
look
look
look
look
look
look
look
look
look
look
look'd
look'd
looking
looking
looking
looks
looks
looks
looks
looks
looks
looks
looks
looks
looks
looks
looks
lord
lords
lords'
lose
lose
lose
lose
lose
lose
lose
lose
lose
losing
losing
losing
loss
loss
loss
loss
loss
loss
loss
loss
losses

| | | |
|---|---|---|
| lost | love | love |
| lost | love | love |
| lost | love | love |
| lost | love | love |
| loud | love | love |
| lov'd | love | love |
| lov'd | love | love |
| lov'd | love | love |
| lov'd | love | love |
| lov'd | love | love |
| Love | love | love |
| Love | love | love |
| love | love | love |
| love | love | love |
| love | love | love |
| love | love | love |
| love | love | love |
| love | love | love |
| love | love | love |
| love | love | love |
| love | love | love |
| love | love | love |
| love | love | love |
| love | love | love |
| love | love | love |
| love | love | love |
| love | love | love |
| love | love | love |
| love | love | love |
| love | love | love |
| love | love | love |
| love | love | love |
| love | love | love |
| love | love | love |
| love | love | love |
| love | love | love |
| love | love | love |
| love | love | love |
| love | love | love |
| love | love | love |
| love | love | love |
| love | love | love |
| love | love | love |
| love | love | love |
| love | love | love |
| love | love | love |
| love | love | love |
| love | love | love |
| love | love | love |
| love | love | love |
| love | love | love |

love
love
love
love
love
love
love
love
love
love
love
love
love
love
love
love
love
love
love
love-god
love-kindling
loveliness
lovely
lovely
lovely
lovely
lovely
lovely
lovely
lovely
lover
lover's
lovers
lovers
lovers'
Love's
Love's
Love's
Love's
Love's
Love's
love's
love's
love's
love's
love's
love's
love's
love's
love's
love's

love's
love's
love's
love's
love's
love's
love's
love's
love's
love's
love's
loves
loves
loves
loves
loves
loves
loves
loves
loves
love-suit
loving
loving
loving
loving
loving
loving
loving
loving
loving
lov'st
lov'st
lov'st
lov'st
lov'st
lov'st
low
low'rst
luck
lust
lust
lusty
lusty
lying

mad
mad
mad
mad
mad
mad
mad

madding
made
made
made
made
made
made
made
made
made
made
made
made
made
made
made
made
made
made
madness
maid
maiden
maiden
maiden
main
main
main
maintain
majesty
majesty
make
make
make
make
make
make
make
make
make
make
make
make
make
make
make
make
make
make
make
make
make

| | | |
|---|---|---|
| make | man | May |
| make | man | may |
| make | manner | may |
| make | manners | may |
| make | manners | may |
| make | manners | may |
| make | man's | may |
| make | man's | may |
| make | mansion | may |
| make | mansion | may |
| make | many | may |
| make | many | may |
| make | many | may |
| make | many | may |
| make | many | may |
| make | many | may |
| make | many | may |
| make | many | may |
| make | many | may |
| make | many | may |
| make | many | may |
| make | many | may |
| makeless | many | may |
| makes | many's | may |
| makes | map | may |
| makes | map | may |
| makes | mar | may |
| makes | marble | may |
| makes | march | may |
| makes | marigold | mayst |
| makes | marjoram | mayst |
| maketh | mark | mayst |
| making | mark | mayst |
| making | mark | mayst |
| making | mark | mayst |
| making | marriage | mayst |
| making | married | mayst |
| making | married | mayst |
| making | Mars | mayst |
| making | marvel | mayst |
| making | mask'd | mayst |
| making | mask'd | me |
| making | masked | me |
| making | masonry | me |
| mak'st | master | me |
| mak'st | master-mistress | me |
| maladies | matcheth | me |
| maladies | matter | me |
| man | matter | me |
| man | matter | me |
| man | maturity | me |

me
me
me
me
me
me
me
me
me
me
me
me
me
me
me
me
me
me
me
me
me
me
me
me
me
me
me
me
me
me
me
me
me
me
me
me
me
me
me
me
me
me
me
me
me
me
me
me
me
me
me
me
me
me
me
me
me
me
me
me
me
me
me
me
me
me
me
me
me
me
me
me
me
me
me
me
me
me
me
me
me
me
me
me
me
me
me
me
me
me
me
me
me
me
me
me
me
me
me
me
me
me
me
me
me
me
me
me
me
me
me
me
me
me
me
me
me
me
me
me
me
me
me
me
me
me
me
me
me
me
me
me
me
me
me
me
me
me
me
me
me
me
me
me
me
me
me
me
me
me
me
me
me

| | | |
|---|---|---|
| me | merit | mind |
| meadows | merit | mind |
| means | merit | mind |
| means | merit | mind |
| means | merit | mind |
| meant | merits | mind |
| measur'd | messengers | mind |
| measure | methinks | mind |
| measure | methinks | mind |
| medicine | methinks | mind |
| meditation | methinks | mind |
| meet | methods | mind |
| meet | metre | minded |
| meetness | middle | mind's |
| melancholy | might | minds |
| memorial | might | minds |
| memory | might | minds |
| memory | might | mine |
| memory | might | mine |
| memory | might | mine |
| memory | might | mine |
| memory | might | mine |
| memory | might | mine |
| memory | might | mine |
| men | might | mine |
| men | might | mine |
| men | might | mine |
| men | might | mine |
| men | might | mine |
| men | might | mine |
| men | might | mine |
| men | might | mine |
| men | might | mine |
| men | might | mine |
| men | might | mine |
| men | might | mine |
| men | might | mine |
| men | might | mine |
| men | might | mine |
| mend | might | mine |
| mend | mightier | mine |
| mend | mightst | mine |
| mended | mightst | mine |
| men's | miles | mine |
| men's | miles | mine |
| men's | million'd | mine |
| men's | millions | mine |
| men's | mind | mine |
| men's | mind | mine |
| merchandiz'd | mind | mine |
| mercy | mind | mine |

| | | |
|---|---|---|
| mine | moan | more |
| mine | moan | more |
| mine | moan | more |
| mine | moan | more |
| mine | moan | more |
| mine | mock | more |
| mine | mock | more |
| mine | mock | more |
| mine | modern | more |
| mine | moiety | more |
| mine | moment | more |
| mine | monarch's | more |
| mine | monsters | more |
| mine | monument | more |
| mine | monument | more |
| mine | monuments | more |
| mine | moods | more |
| mine | moon | more |
| mine | moon | more |
| mine | moon | more |
| mine | more | more |
| mine | more | more |
| mine | more | more |
| mine | more | more |
| mine | more | more |
| mine | more | more |
| mine | more | more |
| mine | more | more |
| minion | more | more |
| minutes | more | more |
| minutes | more | more |
| minutes | more | more |
| minutes | more | more |
| miracle | more | morn |
| miscall'd | more | morn |
| miser | more | morning |
| misplac'd | more | morning |
| misprision | more | morrow |
| miss'd | more | mortal |
| mistake | more | mortal |
| mistaking | more | mortal |
| mistress | more | mortal |
| mistress | more | mortal |
| mistress | more | mortality |
| mistress' | more | mortgag'd |
| mistress' | more | most |
| mistress' | more | most |
| mistress' | more | most |
| mistress' | more | most |
| misuse | more | most |
| mix'd | more | most |

| | | |
|---|---|---|
| most | much | must |
| most | much | must |
| most | much | must |
| most | much | must |
| most | much | must |
| most | much | must |
| most | much | must |
| most | much | must |
| most | much | must |
| most | much | must |
| most | much | must |
| most | much | must |
| most | much | mute |
| most | much | mute |
| most | much | mutual |
| most | mud | mutual |
| most | murderous | my |
| most | murderous | my |
| most | murderous | my |
| most | Muse | my |
| most | Muse | my |
| mother | Muse | my |
| mother | Muse | my |
| mother's | Muse | my |
| mother's | Muse | my |
| mother's | Muse | my |
| motion | muse | my |
| motion | muse | my |
| motion | muse | my |
| motion | muse | my |
| motion | muse | my |
| motley | muse | my |
| mountain | muse | my |
| mountain-tops | muse | my |
| mounted | muse | my |
| mourn | muses | my |
| mourn | music | my |
| mourn | music | my |
| mourners | music | my |
| mourners | music | my |
| mournful | music | my |
| mourning | music | my |
| mourning | must | my |
| mouthed | must | my |
| mouths | must | my |
| move | must | my |
| moving | must | my |
| moving | must | my |
| mow | must | my |
| much | must | my |
| much | must | my |

my
my
my
my
my
my
my
my
my
my
my
my
my
my
my
my
my
my
my
my
my
my
my
my
my
my
my
my
my
my
my
my
my
my
my
my
my
my
my
my
my
my
my
my
my
my
my
my
my
my
my
my
my
my
my
my
my
my
my
my
my
my
my
my
my
my
my
my
my
my
my
my
my
my
my
my
my
my
my
my
my
my
my
my
my
my
my
my
my
my
my
my
my
my
my
my
my
my
my
my
my
my
my
my
my
my
my
my
my
my
my
my
my
my
my
my
my
my
my
my
my
my
my
my
my
my
my
my
my
my
my
my
my
my
my
my
my
my
my
my
my
my
my
my
my
my
my
my
my
my
my
my
my

my my my
my my my
my my my
my my my
my my my
my my my
my my my
my my my
my my my
my my my
my my my
my my my
my my my
my my my
my my my
my my my
my my my
my my my
my my my
my my my
my my my
my my my
my my my
my my my
my my my
my my my
my my my
my my my
my my my
my my my
my my my
my my my
my my my
my my my
my my my
my my my
my my my
my my my
my my my
my my my
my my my
my my my
my my my
my my my
my my my
my my my
my my my
my my my
my my my
my my my
my my my

my
my
my
my
my
my
my
my
my
my
my
my
my
my
my
my
my
my
my
my
my
my
myself
myself
myself
myself
myself
myself
myself
myself
myself
myself
myself
myself
myself
myself
myself
myself
myself
myself
myself
myself
myself
myself
myself
myself
myself
myself
myself
myself
myself

naked
name
name
name
name
name
name
name
name
name
name
name
name
name
name
name
name
name
naming
nativity
Nature
Nature
Nature
Nature
Nature
nature
nature
nature
nature
nature
nature's
nature's
nature's
nature's
nature's
nature's
nay
nay
near
near
near
near
nearly
necessary
neck
need
need
need
need
need

needing
needs
needs
needs
needs
needs
need'st
needy
ne'er
ne'er
ne'er
ne'er-cloying
neglect
neglect
neglected
neigh
neither
neither
nerves
never
never
never
never
never
never
never
never
never
never
never
never
never
never
never
never-resting
new
new
new
new
new
new
new
new
new
new
new
new
new
new
new
new

| | | |
|---|---|---|
| new | no | no |
| new | no | no |
| new | no | no |
| new | no | no |
| new | no | no |
| new-appearing | no | no |
| newer | no | no |
| newer | no | no |
| new-fangled | no | no |
| new-fir'd | no | no |
| new-found | no | no |
| new-made | no | no |
| news | no | no |
| next | no | no |
| next | no | no |
| niggard | no | no |
| niggard | no | no |
| niggarding | no | no |
| night | no | no |
| night | no | no |
| night | no | no |
| night | no | no |
| night | no | no |
| night | no | no |
| night | no | nobler |
| night | no | none |
| night | no | none |
| night | no | none |
| night | no | none |
| night | no | none |
| night | no | none |
| night | no | none |
| night | no | none |
| night | no | none |
| night | no | none |
| night | no | none |
| night | no | none |
| night | no | none |
| night | no | noon |
| night | no | nor |
| nightly | no | nor |
| nightly | no | nor |
| nights | no | nor |
| nights | no | nor |
| nimble | no | nor |
| nimble | no | nor |
| nine | no | nor |
| no | no | nor |
| no | no | nor |
| no | no | nor |
| no | no | nor |

| | | |
|---|---|---|
| nor | not | not |
| nor | not | not |
| nor | not | not |
| nor | not | not |
| nor | not | not |
| nor | not | not |
| nor | not | not |
| nor | not | not |
| nor | not | not |
| nor | not | not |
| nor | not | not |
| nor | not | not |
| nor | not | not |
| nor | not | not |
| nor | not | not |
| nor | not | not |
| nor | not | not |
| nor | not | not |
| nor | not | not |
| nor | not | not |
| nor | not | not |
| nor | not | not |
| nor | not | not |
| nor | not | not |
| nor | not | not |
| nor | not | not |
| nor | not | not |
| nor | not | not |
| nor | not | not |
| nor | not | not |
| nor | not | not |
| nor | not | not |
| nor | not | not |
| nor | not | not |
| nor | not | not |
| nor | not | not |
| nor | not | not |
| nor | not | not |
| nor | not | not |
| nor | not | not |
| nor | not | not |
| not | not | not |
| not | not | not |
| not | not | not |
| not | not | not |
| not | not | not |
| not | not | not |
| not | not | not |
| not | not | not |
| not | not | not |
| not | not | not |

not
not
not
not
not
not
not
not
not
not
not
not
not
not
not
not
not
not
not
not
not
not
not
not
not
not
not
not
not
not
not
not
not
not
not
not
not
not
not
not
not
not
not
not
not
not
not
not
not
not
not

not
not
not
note
note
noted
noted
nothing
nothing
nothing
nothing
nothing
nothing
nothing
nothing
nothing
nothing
nothing
nothing
nothing
nothing
nothing
nothing
nothing
nothing
nothing
nought
nought
nought
nourish'd
novel
now
now
now
now
now
now
now
now
now
now
now
now
now
now
now
now
now
now
now
now

now
now
now
now
now
now
now
now
now
now
now
now
now
now
now
now
now
now
now
now
now
now
now
now
now
number
number
number
numbers
numbers
numbers
numbers
nurs'd
nurse
nurseth
nymphs

O
O
O
O
O
O
O
O
O
O
O
O
O
O

| | | |
|---|---|---|
| O | odour | of |
| O | odour | of |
| O | odours | of |
| O | o'er | of |
| O | o'er | of |
| O | o'er | of |
| O | o'er | of |
| O | o'er | of |
| O | o'er | of |
| O | o'ercharg'd | of |
| O | o'ergreen | of |
| O | o'erlook | of |
| O | o'erpress'd | of |
| O | o'er-read | of |
| O | o'ersnow'd | of |
| O | o'ersways | of |
| O | o'ertake | of |
| O | o'erworn | of |
| O | of | of |
| O | of | of |
| O | of | of |
| O | of | of |
| O | of | of |
| O | of | of |
| O | of | of |
| O | of | of |
| O | of | of |
| O | of | of |
| O | of | of |
| O | of | of |
| O | of | of |
| O | of | of |
| O | of | of |
| O | of | of |
| O | of | of |
| O | of | of |
| oaths | of | of |
| oaths | of | of |
| oaths | of | of |
| oaths' | of | of |
| object | of | of |
| objects | of | of |
| objects | of | of |
| oblation | of | of |
| oblivion | of | of |
| obsequious | of | of |
| obsequious | of | of |
| ocean | of | of |
| ocean | of | of |
| ocean | of | of |
| odour | of | of |

| | | |
|---|---|---|
| of | of | of |
| of | of | of |
| of | of | of |
| of | of | of |
| of | of | of |
| of | of | of |
| of | of | of |
| of | of | of |
| of | of | of |
| of | of | of |
| of | of | of |
| of | of | of |
| of | of | of |
| of | of | of |
| of | of | of |
| of | of | of |
| of | of | of |
| of | of | of |
| of | of | of |
| of | of | of |
| of | of | of |
| of | of | of |
| of | of | of |
| of | of | of |
| of | of | of |
| of | of | of |
| of | of | of |
| of | of | of |
| of | of | of |
| of | of | of |
| of | of | of |
| of | of | of |
| of | of | of |
| of | of | of |
| of | of | of |
| of | of | of |
| of | of | of |
| of | of | of |
| of | of | of |
| of | of | of |
| of | of | of |
| of | of | of |
| of | of | of |
| of | of | of |
| of | of | of |
| of | of | of |
| of | of | of |
| of | of | of |
| of | of | of |
| of | of | of |
| of | of | of |

of
of
of
of
of
of
of
of
of
of
of
of
of
of
of
of
of
of
of
of
of
of
of
of
of
of
of
of
of
of
of
of
of
of
of
of
of
of
of
of
of
of
of
of
of
of
of
of
of
of
of
of
of
of
of
of
of
of
of
of
of
of
of
of
of
of
of
of
of
of
of
of
of
of
of
of
of
of
of
of
of
of
of
of
of
of
of
of
of
of
of
of
of
of
of
of
of
of
of
of
of
of
of
of
of
of
of
of
of
of
of
of
of
of
of
of
of
of
of
of
of
of
of
of
of
of
of
of
of
of
of
off
off
offence
offence
offence's
offences
offend
offender's
offenders
office
offices
oft
oft
oft
oft
oft
often
often
old
old

old
old
old
old
old
old
old
old
old
old
old
old
old
old
old
old
old
old
old
old
older
olives
on
on
on
on
on
on
on
on
on
on
on
on
on
on
on
on
on
on
on
on
on
on
on
on
on
on
on
on
on
on
on
on
on
on
on
on
on
on
on
on
on
on
on
on
on
on
on
on
on
on
on
on
on
on
on
on
on
on
on
on
on
on
on
on
on
on
on
on
on
on
on
on
on
on
on
on
on
on
on
on
on
on
on
on
on
on
once
once
once
once
once
once
once
once
once
once
one
one
one
one
one
one
one
one
one
one
one
one
one
one
one
one
one
one
one
one
one
one
one
one
one
one
one
one
one
one
one
one
one
one
one
one
one
one
one
one
one

one
one's
only
only
only
only
only
only
onset
onward
onwards
open
open
oppress'd
oppress'd
oppression
or
or
or
or
or
or
or
or
or
or
or
or
or
or
or
or
or
or
or
or
or
or
or
or
or
or
or
or
or
or
or
or
or
or
or
or
or
or
or
or
or
or
or
or
or
or
or
or
or
or
or
or
or
or
or
or
or
or
or
or
or
or
or
or
or
or
or
or
or
or
ordering
orient
ornament
ornament
ornament
ornament
ornament
ornaments
orphans
other
other
other
other
other
other
other
other
other
other
other
other
other
other
other
other's
others
others
others
others
others
others
others
others
others
others
others
others'
others'
others'
others'
our
our
our
our
our
our
our
our
our
our
our
our
our
our
our
our
our

our
out
out
out
out
out
out
out
out
out
out
out
out
out
out
out
out
outbraves
outcast
outgoing
outlive
outlive
outlive
outright
outstripp'd
outward
outward
outward
outward
outward
outward
outward
outworn
outworn
over
over-goes
over-partial
over-plus
overthrow
overturn
owe
owes
owest
own
own
own
own
own
own
own
own

own
own
own
own
own
own
own
own
own
own
own
own
own
own
own
own
own
own
own
own
own
own
owner's
owners

pace
pace
pace
page
paid
pain
pain
pain
pain
pain
painful
painted
painted
painted
painted
painted
painter
painter
painter's
painting
painting
painting
painting
painting
painting
palate

palate
pale
pale
paper
papers
parallels
pardon
part
part
part
part
part
part
part
part
part
part
part
part
part
part
part
part
part
part
part
part
partake
particulars
partly
parts
parts
parts
parts
parts
parts
parts
party
pass
pass
pass
pass'd
pass'd
passion
past
past
past
past
past
past
past

past
past
patience
patience
patient
patient
pattern
pattern
paws
pay
pay
pay
paying
pays
pays
peace
peace
pearl
pebbled
peep
pen
pen
pen
pen
pen
pen
pen
pen
pen
pen
penance
pencil
pencil
pent
pent
penury
perceiv'd
perceive
perceiv'st
perfect
perfect
perfection
perfection
perfect'st
perforce
perfumed
perfumes
perfumes
perhaps
perish
perjur'd
perjur'd
perjur'd
permit
perpetual
perpetual
perspective
persuade
perusal
petty
phial
Philomel
phoenix
phrase
physic
physic
physician
physicians
pictur'd
picture
picture
picture
picture's
pierc'd
pilgrimage
pilgrimage
pine
pine
pine
pipe
pitch
pitch
pitied
pitiful
pity
pity
pity
pity
pity
pity
pity
pity
pitying
pity-wanting
place
place
place
place
place
place
place
place
place
place
placed
plague
plague
plague
plagues
plain
plants
play
play
play
play
play
play'd
play'st
plea
plea
plea
plead
plead
pleasant
please
please
please
please
pleased
pleasing
pleasing
pleasure
pleasure
pleasure
pleasure
pleasure
pleasure
pleasure
pleasure
pleasure
pleasure
pleasure
pleasures
plight
plods
plot
pluck
pluck
pluck
pluck
poesy
poet
poet

poet's
poet's
poets
poets
point
point
pointing
points
poison
poison'd
policy
policy
polish'd
politic
pomp
poor
poor
poor
poor
poor
poor
poor
poor
poor
poor
poor
poor
poor
poor
poor
poorly
possess'd
possess'd
possesseth
possessing
possessing
possession
possession
posterity
posterity
posterity
posting
potions
potions
pour'st
poverty
poverty
power
power
power
power

power
power
power
power
power
powerful
powerful
powers
prais'd
prais'd
praise
praise
praise
praise
praise
praise
praise
praise
praise
praise
praise
praise
praise
praise
praise
praise
praise
praise
praise
praise
praise
praise
praise
praise
praise
praise
praise
praise
praises
praises
praises
praises
praising
praising
pray
prayers
precious
precious
precious
precious
precious

predict
prefiguring
prepare
prepare
preposterously
presage
presagers
prescriptions
presence
presence
present
present
present
present
present
present-absent
presenteth
presents
present'st
preserve
press
presume
pretty
pretty
pretty
prevail'd
prevent
prevent'st
prey
prey
prick'd
pride
pride
pride
pride
pride
pride
pride
pride
pride
pride
pride
prime
prime
prime
prime
princes
princes
princes'
print
prison

prisoner
private
privilege
privilege
prize
prize
prize
prizing
proceed
proceeds
process
proclaims
profan'd
profan'd
profane
profit
profitless
profound
prognosticate
progress
promise
prone
proof
proof
proof
prophecies
prophetic
propos'd
proud
proud
proud
proud
proud
proud
proud
proud
proud
proud
proud
proud
prouder
proudest
proudly
proud-pied
prov'd
prov'd
prov'd
prove
prove
prove
prove
prove
prove
prove
prove
prove
prove
prove
prove
prove
proves
provide
proving
provoke
pry
public
public
public
public
publish
pupil
pure
pure
purest
purge
purging
purity
purple
purpos'd
purpose
purpose
purpose
purpose
purpose
pursuing
pursuit
pursuit
put
put
put
put
put
put
put
puts
putt'st
pyramids

qualify
quality
queen
quenched
quest
quest
question
question
quick
quick
quick
quicker
quickly
quiet
quietus
quill
quill
quite
quite
quite
quite
quite

race
rack
rage
rage
rage
rage
rage
ragged
raiment
rain
rain
rain
rainy
rais'd
random
rang'd
rank
rank
rank
rank
rank
ranks
ransom
ransom
ransoms
rare
rare
rare
rare
rarities
rather
raven

raz'd
razed
read
read
read
read
read
reap
rearward
reason
reason
reason
reason
reason
reason
reasons
reasons
reasons
rebel
rebuk'd
receipt
receive
receives
receives
receives
receivest
receiving
receiv'st
receiv'st
recite
reckon
reckon'd
reckoning
recompense
record
record
record
records
recounting
recur'd
red
red
red
red
redeem
reeks
reeleth
refigur'd
refuse
refusest
region
register
registers
rehearse
rehearse
rehearse
rehearse
reign
reign
reign'd
reigns
releasing
relief
religious
remain
remain
remain
remains
remedy
remedy
remember
remember
remember'd
remember'd
remember'd
remembered
remembrance
remembrance
remote
remov'd
remov'd
remov'd
remov'd
remove
remove
remover
render
render
renew
renew'd
renewest
rent
rents
repair
repair
repair
repay
repent
replete
replete
report
report
report
report
repose
repose
reproach
reproving
require
resemble
resembling
resembling
reserve
reserve
resort
respect
respect
respect
respect
respects
rest
rest
rest
rest
rest
rest
restful
restor'd
restore
resty
re-survey
retention
return
return
return
return
return
return
return'd
revenge
revenues
review
reviewest
revolt
revolution
rhetoric
rhyme
rhyme
rhyme
rhyme
rhyme
rhyme
rhymers

rich
rich
rich
rich
rich
rich
rich
rich
rich
rich
richer
riches
riches
richly
rich-proud
rid
ride
ride
ride
rider
right
right
right
right
right
right
right
right
right
right
rightly
rights
rigour
riot
ripe
riper
riper
rise
rise
rising
rite
robb'd
robbery
robbery
robbing
robe
robs
robs
rocks
rolling
rondure
roof
room
root
root
rose
rose
rose
rose
rose
rose
roses
roses
roses
roses
roses
roses
roses
rosy
rotten
rotten
rough
rude
rude
rude
rude
rudely
rud'st
ruin
ruinate
ruin'd
ruin'd
ruining
ruminate
run
runn'st
runs
ruth

sable
sacred
sacred
sad
sad
sad
sad
sad
sad
sad
sadly
said
said
said
said
sail
sail
sail
saint
saith
sake
sake
sake
sake
sake
sake
sake
sake
salutation
salve
salve
salving
same
same
same
same
same
same
sang
sap
sap
satire
Saturn
sauces
saucy
saucy
savage
sav'd
save
save
save
save
save
save
save
save
savour
saw
saw
saw
saw
saw
say
say

say
say
say
say
say
say
say
say
say
say
say
say
say
say
say
say
say
say
say
say
say
say
say
say
say
say
saying
says
says
says
says
says
scandal
scanted
scap'd
scarcely
scarlet
scope
scope
scope
scope
scope
score
scorn
scorn
scorn'd
scythe
scythe
scythe
scythe
sea
sea
sea
sea
seal
seal'd
seals
sea's
seasons
seasons
seasons'
seat
seat
second
second
second
second
seconds
secret
see
see
see
see
see
see
see
see
see
see
see
see
see
see
see
see
see
see
see
see
see
see
see
see
see
see
see
see
see
see
see
see
see
see
see
seeing
seeing
seeing
seeing
seeing
seeing
seek
seek
seek
seek
seeking
seem
seem
seem
seem
seem
seem
seem
seem
seem
seem
seem
seem
seem'd
seem'd
seem'd
seeming
seeming
seeming
seemly
seems
seems
seen
seen
seen
seen
seen
seen
seen
seen
seen
seen
seen
sees
seest
seest
seething
seldom
seldom

self
self
self
self
self
self
self
self
self
self
self-doing
self-example
self-kill'd
self-love
self-love
self-love
self-loving
self-same
self-substantial
self-will'd
sell
selling
semblance
send
send
send'st
sense
sense
sense
sense
senses
sensual
sensual
separable
separation
sepulchres
sequent
servant
servant's
service
services
serving
serving
sessions
set
set
set
set
set
set
set
sets
sets
settled
several
shade
shade
shade
shade
shadow
shadow
shadow
shadow
shadow
shadow
shadow
shadow's
shadows
shadows
shadows
shady
shake
shake
shake
shaken
shaken
shall
shall
shall
shall
shall
shall
shall
shall
shall
shall
shall
shall
shall
shall
shall
shall
shall
shall
shall
shall
shall
shall
shall
shall
shall
shall
shall
shall
shall
shall
shall
shall
shall
shall
shall
shall
shall
shall
shall
shall
shall
shall
shall
shall
shall
shall
shall
shall
shall
shall
shall
shall
shall
shall
shall
shall
shall
shall
shall
shall
shall
shall
shall
shallowest
shalt
shalt
shalt
shalt
shalt
shalt
shalt
shalt
shalt
shalt
shalt
sham'd
shame
shame
shame
shame
shame

| | | |
|---|---|---|
| shame | she | should |
| shame | sheaves | should |
| shame | sheds | should |
| shame | shifting | should |
| shame | shifts | should |
| shamefully | shine | should |
| shames | shine | should |
| shames | shine | should |
| shape | shine | should |
| shape | shines | should |
| shape | shines | should |
| shape | shook | should |
| shape | shoot | should |
| shapes | shop | should |
| share | shore | should |
| sharp | shore | should |
| sharpen'd | shore | shouldst |
| sharp'st | shorn | shouldst |
| she | short | shouldst |
| she | short | shouldst |
| she | short | shouldst |
| she | short | shouldst |
| she | short-number'd | show |
| she | should | show |
| she | should | show |
| she | should | show |
| she | should | show |
| she | should | show |
| she | should | show |
| she | should | show |
| she | should | show |
| she | should | show |
| she | should | show |
| she | should | show |
| she | should | show |
| she | should | show |
| she | should | show |
| she | should | show |
| she | should | show |
| she | should | show |
| she | should | show |
| she | should | show |
| she | should | show |
| she | should | show |
| she | should | show |
| she | should | showers |
| she | should | showers |
| she | should | showing |
| she | should | shown |
| she | should | shown |
| she | should | shows |

shows
shows
shows
shows
shows
show'st
shun
shun
sick
sick
sick
sick
sick
sick
sicken
sickle
sickle's
sickly
sickness
side
side
side
side
side
sides
siege
sigh
sighs
sight
sight
sight
sight
sight
sight
sight
sight
sight
sight
sight
sight
sight
sight
sight
sight
sight
sightless
sightless
signs
silence
silence
silence
silent
silent
silver
silver'd
simple
simple
simple
simplicity
simply
sin
sin
sin
sin
sin
sin
sin
sin
since
since
since
since
since
since
since
since
since
since
since
since
since
since
since
since
since
since
since
since
since
sinful
sinful
sinful
sing
sing
sing
sing
sing
sing
sing
single
single
single
single
singleness
sings
sings
sinks
sins
sins
sins
sire
Siren
sit
sit
sits
situation
skill
skill
skill
skill
skill
skill
skill
skill
sky
slain
slain
slander
slander
slander'd
slanderers
slandering
slander's
slave
slave
slave
slave
slave
slave
slavery
slay
sleep
sleep
sleep
sleep
sleeping
slept
slide
slight
slight
slow

| | | |
|---|---|---|
| slow | so | so |
| slow | so | so |
| slow | so | so |
| slow | so | so |
| slumbers | so | so |
| sluttish | so | so |
| small | so | so |
| small | so | so |
| smell | so | so |
| smell | so | so |
| smell | so | so |
| smell | so | so |
| smells | so | so |
| smiling | so | so |
| smoke | so | so |
| smother | so | so |
| snow | so | so |
| so | so | so |
| so | so | so |
| so | so | so |
| so | so | so |
| so | so | so |
| so | so | so |
| so | so | so |
| so | so | so |
| so | so | so |
| so | so | so |
| so | so | so |
| so | so | so |
| so | so | so |
| so | so | so |
| so | so | so |
| so | so | so |
| so | so | so |
| so | so | so |
| so | so | so |
| so | so | so |
| so | so | so |
| so | so | so |
| so | so | so |
| so | so | so |
| so | so | so |
| so | so | so |
| so | so | so |
| so | so | so |
| so | so | so |
| so | so | so |
| so | so | so |
| so | so | so |
| so | so | so |
| so | so | so |

| | | |
|---|---|---|
| so | sometime | sourest |
| so | sometime | sourly |
| so | sometime | sourly |
| so | sometime | sovereign |
| so | sometime | sovereign |
| so | sometimes | sovereign |
| so | son | sovereign |
| so | son | space |
| so | son | spacious |
| sober | song | sparkling |
| society | song | speak |
| soft | song | speak |
| soil | song | speak |
| sold | songs | speak |
| sole | soon | speak |
| solemn | soon | speak |
| solve | soon | speak |
| some | sooner | speak |
| some | sooner | speaking |
| some | sorrow | speaking |
| some | sorrow | speaking |
| some | sorrow | speaking |
| some | sorrow | special |
| some | sorrow | special-blest |
| some | sorrows | speechless |
| some | sorrows | speechless |
| some | sorry | speed |
| some | sort | speed |
| some | sort | speed |
| some | sought | spend |
| some | soul | spend |
| some | soul | spend |
| some | soul | spend |
| some | soul | spend |
| some | soul | spending |
| some | soul | spends |
| some | soul | spend'st |
| some | soul | spent |
| some | soul | spent |
| some | soul | spent |
| some | soul's | spent |
| some | soul's | spent |
| some | souls | spent |
| some | souls | spheres |
| some | sound | spies |
| some | sound | spirit |
| some | soundless | spirit |
| some | sounds | spirit |
| something | sounds | spirit |
| something | sour | spirit |
| sometime | sour | spirit |

| | | |
|---|---|---|
| spirit | star | stell'd |
| spirit | stars | stern |
| spirit | stars | stewards |
| spirit | stars | stick'st |
| spirits | stars | still |
| spirits | stars | still |
| spite | starved | still |
| spite | state | still |
| spite | state | still |
| spite | state | still |
| spite | state | still |
| spites | state | still |
| splendour | state | still |
| spoil | state | still |
| spoils | state | still |
| sport | state | still |
| sport | state | still |
| sportive | state | still |
| spot | state | still |
| spread | state | still |
| spring | state | still |
| spring | statues | still |
| spring | statute | still |
| spring | stay | still |
| spring | stay | still |
| springs | stay | still |
| spur | stay | still |
| spur | stay | still |
| spurring | stay | still |
| stage | stay | still |
| stage | stay | still |
| stain | stay | still |
| stain | stays | still |
| stain | steal | still |
| stain'd | steal | still |
| staineth | steal | still |
| stamp | steal | still |
| stamp'd | steal | still |
| stand | steal | still |
| stand | steal | still |
| stand | stealing | still |
| stand | stealing | still |
| stand | steals | still |
| stand | stealth | still |
| stand | steel | still |
| stand | steel | stirr'd |
| stands | steel | stole |
| stands | steel'd | stolen |
| stands | steep | stolen |
| star | steep-up | stolen |
| star | steepy | stolen |

stolen
stone
stone
stone
stones
stop
stop
stopped
stops
store
store
store
store
store
store
store
store
store
stores
stores'
storm-beaten
stormy
story
story
story
story
stout
straight
straight
straight
straight
straight
straight
straight
strained
strains
strange
strange
strange
strange
strange
strange
strangely
strangely
strangle
straying
streams
strength
strength
strength
strength
strength
strength
strengthen'd
strength's
stretched
strife
strikes
string
strive
strive
striving
strong
strong
strong
strong
strong
strong
strong
strong
strong
stronger
stronger
strongly
strongly
struck
strumpeted
style
style
style
subdued
subject
subject
subject
subject
subject
subjects
subjects
suborn'd
subscribes
subsist
substance
substance
substance
substance
subtleties
succeeding
succession
successive
such
such
such
such
such
such
such
such
such
such
such
such
such
such
such
such
such
such
such
such
such
such
such
such
such
such
such
such
such
such
such
such
sue
suffer
suffer
sufferance
suffer'd
suffering
suffers
suffic'd
suggest
suit
suited
sullen
sullen
sullied
sum
sum
sum
sum
summer
summer
summer
summer
summer

summer
summer
summer
summer's
summer's
summer's
summer's
summer's
summer's
summer's
summer's
summer's
summer's
summer's
summers'
summon
sums
sun
sun
sun
sun
sun
sun
sun
sun
sun
sun
sun
sunk
sunken
sun's
suns
sunset
suppos'd
suppose
supposed
supposing
supprest
sure
sure
sure
surety-like
surfeit
surly
surmise
surmount
survey
survey
survive
survive
suspect
suspect
suspect
swallow'd
swart-
complexion'd
sway
sway
sway'st
swear
swear
swear
swear
swear
swear
swear
swearing
swears
sweet
sweet
sweet
sweet
sweet
sweet
sweet
sweet
sweet
sweet
sweet
sweet
sweet
sweet
sweet
sweet
sweet
sweet
sweet
sweet
sweet
sweet
sweet
sweet
sweet
sweet
sweet
sweet
sweet
sweet
sweet
sweet
sweet
sweet
sweet
sweet
sweet
sweet
sweet
sweet
sweet
sweet
sweet
sweet
sweet
sweet
sweet
sweet
sweet
sweet
sweet
sweet
sweet
sweet
sweet
sweet
sweet
sweet
sweet
sweet-beloved
sweetest
sweetest
sweetest
sweetest
sweetest
sweetly
sweetly
sweetness
sweetness
sweets
sweets
sweets
sweets
sweets
sweets
sweet-season'd
sweet'st
swerving
swift
swift
swift
swift
swift-footed
sword
sworn
sworn
sworn
sympathiz'd

table
tables
tables
take
take
take
take
take
take
take
take
take
take
take
take
take
taken
taken
taken
taker
takes
takes
takes
tall
tallies
tame
tan
tann'd
task
taste
taste
taste
taste
tatter'd
tatter'd
taught
taught
taught
taught
taught
taught
teach
teach
teach
teachest
tear
tears
tears
tears
tears
tears

teeming
teeth
tell
tell
tell
tell
tell
tell
tell
tell
tell
tell
tell
tell
tell
tell
tell
telling
tells
tells
temperate
tempests
temptation
temptation
tempteth
tempting
ten
ten
ten
ten
ten
ten
ten
tenants
tend
tend
tend
tender
tender
tender
tender
tender
tender
tender
tender'd
tenor
tenth
term
term'd
terms
testy

th'
than
than
than
than
than
than
than
than
than
than
than
than
than
than
than
than
than
than
than
than
than
than
than
than
than
than
than
than
than
than
than
than
than
than
than
than
than
than
than
than
than
than
than
than
than
than
than
than
thank
thanks

| | | |
|---|---|---|
| that | that | that |
| that | that | that |
| that | that | that |
| that | that | that |
| that | that | that |
| that | that | that |
| that | that | that |
| that | that | that |
| that | that | that |
| that | that | that |
| that | that | that |
| that | that | that |
| that | that | that |
| that | that | that |
| that | that | that |
| that | that | that |
| that | that | that |
| that | that | that |
| that | that | that |
| that | that | that |
| that | that | that |
| that | that | that |
| that | that | that |
| that | that | that |
| that | that | that |
| that | that | that |
| that | that | that |
| that | that | that |
| that | that | that |
| that | that | that |
| that | that | that |
| that | that | that |
| that | that | that |
| that | that | that |
| that | that | that |
| that | that | that |
| that | that | that |
| that | that | that |
| that | that | that |
| that | that | that |
| that | that | that |
| that | that | that |
| that | that | that |
| that | that | that |
| that | that | that |
| that | that | that |
| that | that | that |
| that | that | that |
| that | that | that |
| that | that | that |
| that | that | that |

| | | |
|---|---|---|
| that | that | that |
| that | that | that |
| that | that | that |
| that | that | that |
| that | that | that |
| that | that | that |
| that | that | that |
| that | that | that |
| that | that | that |
| that | that | that |
| that | that | that |
| that | that | that |
| that | that | that |
| that | that | that |
| that | that | that |
| that | that | that |
| that | that | that |
| that | that | that |
| that | that | that |
| that | that | that |
| that | that | that |
| that | that | that |
| that | that | that |
| that | that | that |
| that | that | that |
| that | that | that |
| that | that | that |
| that | that | that |
| that | that | that |
| that | that | that |
| that | that | that |
| that | that | that |
| that | that | that |
| that | that | that |
| that | that | that |
| that | that | that |
| that | that | that |
| that | that | that |
| that | that | that |
| that | that | that |
| that | that | that |
| that | that | that |
| that | that | that |
| that | that | that |
| that | that | that |
| that | that | that |
| that | that | that |
| that | that | that |
| that | that | that |
| that | that | that |
| that | that | that |

that
that
that
that
that
that
that
that
that
that
that
that
that
that
that's
the
the
the
the
the
the
the
the
the
the
the
the
the
the
the
the
the
the
the
the
the
the
the
the
the
the
the
the
the
the
the
the
the
the
the
the
the
the
the
the
the
the
the
the
the
the
the
the
the
the
the
the
the
the
the
the
the
the
the
the
the
the
the
the
the
the
the
the
the
the
the
the
the
the
the
the
the
the
the
the
the
the
the
the
the
the
the
the
the
the
the
the
the
the
the
the
the
the
the
the
the
the
the
the
the
the
the
the
the
the
the
the
the
the
the
the
the
the
the
the
the
the
the
the
the
the
the
the
the
the
the
the
the
the
the
the
the
the
the
the
the
the
the
the

the
the
the
the
the
the
the
the
the
the
the
the
the
the
the
the
the
the
the
the
the
the
the
the
the
the
the
the
the
the
the
the
the
the
the
the
the
the
the
the
the
the
the
the
the
the
the
the
the
the
the
the
the
the
the
the
the
the
the
the
the
the
the
the
the
the
the
the
the
the
the
the
the
the
the
the
the
the
the
the
the
the
the
the
the
the
the
the
the
the
the
the
the
the
the
the
the
the
the
the
the
the
the
the
the
the
the
the
the
the
the
the
the
the
the
the
the
the
the
the
the
the
the
the
the
the
the
the
the
the
the
the
the
the
the
the
the
the
the
the
the
the
the
the
the
the
the
the
the
the
the
the
the
the
the
the
the
the
the
the
the
the
the

the the the
the the the
the the the
the the the
the the the
the the the
the the the
the the the
the the the
the the the
the the the
the the the
the the the
the the the
the the the
the the the
the the the
the the the
the the the
the the the
the the the
the the the
the the the
the the the
the the the
the the the
the the the
the the the
the the the
the the the
the the the
the the the
the the the
the the the
the the the
the the the
the the the
the the the
the the the
the the the
the the the
the the the
the the the
the the the
the the the
the the the
the the the
the the the
the the thee
the the thee
the the thee

thee
thee
thee
thee
thee
thee
thee
thee
thee
thee
thee
thee
thee
thee
thee
thee
thee
thee
thee
thee
thee
thee
thee
thee
thee
thee
thee
thee
thee
thee
thee
thee
thee
thee
thee
thee
thee
thee
thee
thee
thee
thee
thee
thee
thee
thee
thee
thee
thee
thee
thee
thee
thee
thee
thee
thee
thee
thee
thee
thee
thee
thee
thee
thee
thee
thee
thee
thee
thee
thee
thee
thee
thee
thee
thee
thee
thee
thee
thee
thee
thee
thee
thee
thee
thee
thee
thee
thee
thee
thee
thee
thee
thee
thee
thee
thee
thee
thee
thee
thee
thee
thee
thee
thee
thee
thee
thee
thee
thee
thee
thee
thee
thee
thee
thee
thee
thee
thee
thee
thee
thee
thee
thee
thee
thee
thee
thee
thee
thee
thee
thee
thee
thee
thee
thee
thee
thee
thee
thee
thee
thee
thee
thee
thee
thee
thee
thee
thee
thee
thee
thee
thee
thee

thee
thee
thee
thee
thee
thee
theft
their
their
their
their
their
their
their
their
their
their
their
their
their
their
their
their
their
their
their
their
their
their
their
their
their
their
their
their
their
their
their
their
their
their
their
their
their
their
their
their
their
their
their
their
their

their
their
their
their
their
their
their
their
their
their
their
their
their
their
their
their
their
their
their
theirs
theirs
them
them
them
them
them
them
them
them
them
them
them
them
them
them
them
them
them
themes
themselves
themselves
themselves
themselves
themselves
themselves
then
then
then
then
then
then

then
then
then
then
then
then
then
then
then
then
then
then
then
then
then
then
then
then
then
then
then
then
then
then
then
then
then
then
then
then
then
then
then
then
then
then
then
then
then
then
then
then
then
then
then
then
then
then
then
then
then

| | | |
|---|---|---|
| then | therefore | they |
| then | therefore | they |
| then | therefore | they |
| then | therefore | they |
| then | therefore | they |
| then | therefore | they |
| then | therefore | they |
| then | therefore | they |
| then | therefore | they |
| then | therefore | they |
| then | therefore | they |
| then | therefore | they |
| then | therein | they |
| then | therein | they |
| then | therein | they |
| then | thereof | they |
| then | there's | they |
| then | these | they |
| thence | these | they |
| thence | these | they |
| thence | these | they |
| thence | these | they |
| thence | these | they |
| thence | these | they |
| thence | these | they |
| thence | these | they |
| there | these | they |
| there | these | they |
| there | these | they |
| there | these | they |
| there | these | they |
| there | these | they |
| there | these | they |
| there | these | they |
| there | these | they |
| there | these | they |
| there | these | they |
| there | these | they |
| there | they | they |
| there | they | they |
| there | they | thief |
| there | they | thief |
| there | they | thief |
| there | they | thief |
| thereby | they | thievish |
| thereby | they | thievish |
| therefore | they | thine |
| therefore | they | thine |
| therefore | they | thine |
| therefore | they | thine |
| therefore | they | thine |

| | | |
|---|---|---|
| thine | thing | this |
| thine | things | this |
| thine | things | this |
| thine | things | this |
| thine | things | this |
| thine | things | this |
| thine | things | this |
| thine | things | this |
| thine | things | this |
| thine | things | this |
| thine | things | this |
| thine | things | this |
| thine | things | this |
| thine | things | this |
| thine | things | this |
| thine | think | this |
| thine | think | this |
| thine | think | this |
| thine | think | this |
| thine | think | this |
| thine | think | this |
| thine | think | this |
| thine | think | this |
| thine | think | this |
| thine | think | this |
| thine | think | this |
| thine | think | this |
| thine | think | this |
| thine | think | this |
| thine | think | this |
| thine | thinking | this |
| thine | thinking | this |
| thine | thinking | this |
| thine | thinks | this |
| thine | thinks | this |
| thine | thinly | this |
| thine | third | this |
| thine | this | this |
| thine | this | this |
| thine | this | this |
| thine | this | this |
| thine | this | this |
| thing | this | this |
| thing | this | this |
| thing | this | this |
| thing | this | this |
| thing | this | this |
| thing | this | this |
| thing | this | this |
| thing | this | this |
| thing | this | this |

this
this
this
this
this
this
this
this
this
this
this
this
this
this
this
this
this
this
this
this
this
this
this
this
this
this
this
this
this
this
this
this
this
this
this
this
this
this
this
this
this
thither
thorns
thorns
thorns
those
those
those
those
those
those

those
those
those
those
those
those
those
those
those
those
those
those
those
those
those
those
those
those
those
those
those
those
those
those
those
those
those
thou
thou
thou
thou
thou
thou
thou
thou
thou
thou
thou
thou
thou
thou
thou
thou
thou
thou
thou
thou
thou
thou
thou
thou

thou
thou
thou
thou
thou
thou
thou
thou
thou
thou
thou
thou
thou
thou
thou
thou
thou
thou
thou
thou
thou
thou
thou
thou
thou
thou
thou
thou
thou
thou
thou
thou
thou
thou
thou
thou
thou
thou
thou
thou
thou
thou
thou
thou
thou
thou
thou
thou
thou
thou
thou

thou thou thou
thou thou thou
thou thou thou
thou thou thou
thou thou thou
thou thou thou
thou thou thou
thou thou thou
thou thou thou
thou thou thou
thou thou thou
thou thou thou
thou thou thou
thou thou thou
thou thou thou
thou thou thou
thou thou thou
thou thou thou
thou thou thou
thou thou thou
thou thou thou
thou thou thou
thou thou thou
thou thou thou
thou thou thou
thou thou thou
thou thou thou
thou thou thou
thou thou thou
thou thou thou
thou thou thou
thou thou thou
thou thou thou
thou thou thou
thou thou thou
thou thou thou
thou thou thou
thou thou thou
thou thou thou
thou thou thou
thou thou thou
thou thou thou
thou thou thou
thou thou thou
thou thou thou
thou thou thou
thou thou thou
thou thou thou
thou thou thou
thou thou thou
thou thou thou

thou
thou
thou
thou
thou
thou
thou
though
though
though
though
though
though
though
though
though
though
though
though
though
though
though
though
though
though
though
though
though
though
though
though
though
though
though
though
though
though
though
though
though
thought
thought
thought
thought
thought
thought
thought
thought
thought
thought
thought

thought
thought
thought
thought
thought
thought
thought
thoughts
thoughts
thoughts
thoughts
thoughts
thoughts
thoughts
thoughts
thoughts
thoughts
thoughts
thoughts
thoughts
thoughts
thoughts
thoughts
thoughts
thoughts
thousand
thousand
thousand
thrall
thralled
three
three
three
three
three
three
three
three-fold
threescore
threw
thrice
thrice
thrice
thriftless
thrive
thrive
thrivers
throned
through
through
through

through
through
through
throw
thrust
thrusts
thunder
thus
thus
thus
thus
thus
thus
thus
thus
thus
thus
thus
thus
thus
thus
thus
thus
thus
thus
thus
thus
thus
thus
thy
thy
thy
thy
thy
thy
thy
thy
thy
thy
thy
thy
thy
thy
thy
thy
thy
thy
thy
thy
thy
thy

thy thy thy
thy thy thy
thy thy thy
thy thy thy
thy thy thy
thy thy thy
thy thy thy
thy thy thy
thy thy thy
thy thy thy
thy thy thy
thy thy thy
thy thy thy
thy thy thy
thy thy thy
thy thy thy
thy thy thy
thy thy thy
thy thy thy
thy thy thy
thy thy thy
thy thy thy
thy thy thy
thy thy thy
thy thy thy
thy thy thy
thy thy thy
thy thy thy
thy thy thy
thy thy thy
thy thy thy
thy thy thy
thy thy thy
thy thy thy
thy thy thy
thy thy thy
thy thy thy
thy thy thy
thy thy thy
thy thy thy
thy thy thy
thy thy thy
thy thy thy
thy thy thy
thy thy thy
thy thy thy
thy thy thy
thy thy thy
thy thy thy
thy thy thy
thy thy thy

| | | |
|---|---|---|
| thy | thy | thyself |
| thy | thy | thyself |
| thy | thy | thyself |
| thy | thy | thyself |
| thy | thy | thyself |
| thy | thy | thyself |
| thy | thy | thyself |
| thy | thy | thyself |
| thy | thy | tickled |
| thy | thy | tie |
| thy | thy | tie |
| thy | thy | tied |
| thy | thy | tiger's |
| thy | thy | till |
| thy | thy | till |
| thy | thy | till |
| thy | thy | till |
| thy | thy | till |
| thy | thy | till |
| thy | thy | till |
| thy | thy | till |
| thy | thy | till |
| thy | thy | till |
| thy | thy | till |
| thy | thy | till |
| thy | thy | till |
| thy | thy | till |
| thy | thy | tillage |
| thy | thy | Time |
| thy | thy | Time |
| thy | thy | Time |
| thy | thy | Time |
| thy | thy | Time |
| thy | thy | Time |
| thy | thy | Time |
| thy | thy | Time |
| thy | thy | Time |
| thy | thy | Time |
| thy | thyself | Time |
| thy | thyself | time |
| thy | thyself | time |
| thy | thyself | time |
| thy | thyself | time |
| thy | thyself | time |
| thy | thyself | time |
| thy | thyself | time |
| thy | thyself | time |
| thy | thyself | time |
| thy | thyself | time |
| thy | thyself | time |
| thy | thyself | time |

| | | |
|---|---|---|
| time | times | to |
| time | times | to |
| time | times | to |
| time | times | to |
| time | times | to |
| time | tincture | to |
| time | tir'd | to |
| time | tir'd | to |
| time | tir'd | to |
| time | tired | to |
| time | tires | to |
| time | 'tis | to |
| time | 'tis | to |
| time | 'tis | to |
| time | 'tis | to |
| time | 'tis | to |
| time | 'tis | to |
| time | 'tis | to |
| time | 'tis | to |
| time | 'tis | to |
| time | 'tis | to |
| time | 'tis | to |
| time | 'tis | to |
| time | title | to |
| time | title | to |
| time | titles | to |
| time | to | to |
| time | to | to |
| time | to | to |
| time | to | to |
| time-bettering | to | to |
| Time's | to | to |
| Time's | to | to |
| Time's | to | to |
| Time's | to | to |
| Time's | to | to |
| Time's | to | to |
| Time's | to | to |
| Time's | to | to |
| Time's | to | to |
| Time's | to | to |
| Time's | to | to |
| Time's | to | to |
| Time's | to | to |
| time's | to | to |
| time's | to | to |
| time's | to | to |
| times | to | to |
| times | to | to |
| times | to | to |
| times | to | to |

| | | |
|---|---|---|
| to | to | to |
| to | to | to |
| to | to | to |
| to | to | to |
| to | to | to |
| to | to | to |
| to | to | to |
| to | to | to |
| to | to | to |
| to | to | to |
| to | to | to |
| to | to | to |
| to | to | to |
| to | to | to |
| to | to | to |
| to | to | to |
| to | to | to |
| to | to | to |
| to | to | to |
| to | to | to |
| to | to | to |
| to | to | to |
| to | to | to |
| to | to | to |
| to | to | to |
| to | to | to |
| to | to | to |
| to | to | to |
| to | to | to |
| to | to | to |
| to | to | to |
| to | to | to |
| to | to | to |
| to | to | to |
| to | to | to |
| to | to | to |
| to | to | to |
| to | to | to |
| to | to | to |
| to | to | to |
| to | to | to |
| to | to | to |
| to | to | to |
| to | to | to |
| to | to | to |
| to | to | to |
| to | to | to |
| to | to | to |
| to | to | to |
| to | to | to |
| to | to | to |

| | | |
|---|---|---|
| to | to | to |
| to | to | to |
| to | to | to |
| to | to | to |
| to | to | to |
| to | to | to |
| to | to | to |
| to | to | to |
| to | to | to |
| to | to | to |
| to | to | to |
| to | to | to |
| to | to | to |
| to | to | to |
| to | to | to |
| to | to | to |
| to | to | to |
| to | to | to |
| to | to | to |
| to | to | to |
| to | to | to |
| to | to | to |
| to | to | to |
| to | to | to |
| to | to | to |
| to | to | to |
| to | to | to |
| to | to | to |
| to | to | to |
| to | to | to |
| to | to | to |
| to | to | to |
| to | to | to |
| to | to | to |
| to | to | to |
| to | to | to |
| to | to | to |
| to | to | to |
| to | to | to |
| to | to | to |
| to | to | to |
| to | to | to |
| to | to | to |
| to | to | to |
| to | to | to |
| to | to | to |
| to | to | to |
| to | to | to |
| to | to | to |
| to | to | to |
| to | to | to |

| | | |
|---|---|---|
| to | tongue | touches |
| to | tongue | touches |
| to | tongue | toward |
| to | tongue | towards |
| to | tongue | towards |
| to | tongue | towers |
| to | tongue | tract |
| to | tongue | traffic |
| to | tongue | transferr'd |
| to | tongue | transfix |
| to | tongue's | transgression |
| to | tongues | translate |
| to | tongues | translated |
| to | tongues | transport |
| to | tongues | travail |
| to | tongue-tied | travel |
| to | tongue-tied | travel |
| to | tongue-tied | travell'd |
| to | tongue-tied | travel's |
| to | too | travels |
| to | too | treads |
| to | too | treason |
| to | too | treasure |
| to | too | treasure |
| to | too | treasure |
| to | too | treasure |
| to | too | treasure |
| to-day | too | treasure |
| to-day | too | treasure |
| to-day | too | treasure |
| together | too | treasure |
| toil | too | trees |
| toil | too | trenches |
| toil | too | trespass |
| toil | too | trespass |
| toil'd | took | tresses |
| told | took | trial |
| told | took | tribes |
| told | took | trifle |
| told | took | trifles |
| tomb | top | trim |
| tomb | torment | trimm'd |
| tomb | torment | tripping |
| tomb | torments | triumph |
| tomb | torn | triumph |
| tomb'd | torture | triumph |
| tombs | torture | triumphant |
| to-morrow | touch | triumphant |
| to-morrow | touch'd | trophies |
| to-morrow | touches | trouble |
| tongue | touches | truant |

true
true
true
true
true
true
true
true
true
true
true
true
true
true
true
true
true
true
true
true
true
true
true
true
true
true
true
true
true
true
true
true
true
true
true
true
true
truest
true-telling
truly
truly
truly
truly
truly
trust
trust
trust
trust
trust
truth
truth

truth
truth
truth
truth
truth
truth
truth
truth
truth
truth
truth
truth
truth
truth
truth
truth
truth
truth
truth
truth
truth
truth's
truths
try
tune
turn
turn
turn
turn
turn'd
turn'd
turns
turns
turns
twain
twain
twain
twenty
twice
twice
twilight
twire
'twixt
'twixt
two
two
two
two
two
two
two

two
two
twofold
tyrannous
tyranny
tyrant
tyrant
tyrant
tyrants
tryants'

ugly
unbless
unbred
uncertain
under
under
under
under
under
under
undivided
unear'd
unfair
unfather'd
unfather'd
unfolding
unhappily
unions
universe
unjust
unkind
unkind
unkind
unkindness
unkindness
unknown
unknown
unlearned
unless
unless
unless
unless
unless
unless
unlettered
unlook'd
unlook'd
unmoved
unperfect
unprovident

unrespected
unrespected
unrest
unseeing
unseen
unseen
unset
unstained
unsway'd
unswept
untainted
unthrift
unthrifts
unthrifty
until
unto
untold
untrimm'd
untrue
untrue
untutor'd
unus'd
unus'd
unus'd
unused
unwoo'd
unworthiness
up
up
up
up
up
up
up
up
up
up
up
up
up
up
up
uphold
up-locked
upon
upon
upon
upon
upon
upon
upon
upon
upon
upon
upon
upon
upon
upon
upon
upon
upon
upon
upon
upon
upon
upon
upon
upon
upon
upon
upon
upon
upon
uprear
urge
urge
us
us
us'd
use
use
use
use
use
use
use
use
use
use
use
use
use
used
used
user
usest
ushers
usurer
usurer
usury
utmost
uttering
vacant
vainly
vainly
valley-fountain
vanish'd
vanish'd
vanishing
vantage
variation
varying
vassal
vassal
vassalage
vaunt
veil
veins
veins
vengeful
verdict
vermilion
verse
verse
verse
verse
verse
verse
verse
verse
verse
verse
verse
verse
verse
verse
verse
verses
very
very
very
very
very
very
very
vex
vex
vex'd
vice
vices
victor
victories

victors
view
view
view
view
view
view
view
view
viewest
vile
vile
vile
vilest
violet
violet
virgin
virtue
virtue
virtue
virtue
virtue
virtue
virtue
virtuous
virtuous
virtuous
visage
vision
voice
voices
votary
vouchsafe
vouchsafe
vow
vow
vow'd
vowing
vows
vows
vulgar
vulgar
vulgar

wail
wail
wailing
wait
wait
waiting
wake
waken'd
waking
walk
walks
walks
walls
walls
wandering
wander'st
wane
waning
want
want
want
want
wanting
wanting
wanton
wantonly
wantonness
war
war
war
war
war
war
ward
wardrobe
wards
warm
warm'd
warning
warrantise
warrior
war's
wary
was
was
was
was
was
was
was
was
was
was
was
was
was
was
was
was
was
was
was
was
was
was
was
was
was
was
was
was
was
was
was
was
was
waste
waste
waste
waste
waste
waste
waste
wasted
wasteful
wasteful
wastes
wastes
watch
watch
watching
watchman
water
water
water
water
water
wat'ry
waves
way
way
way
way
way
way
we
we
we
we
we
we
we
we

| | | |
|---|---|---|
| we | well | west |
| we | well | west |
| we | well | wet |
| we | well | what |
| we | well | what |
| we | well | what |
| we | well | what |
| weak | well | what |
| weak | well | what |
| weakens | well | what |
| weakness | well | what |
| wealth | well | what |
| wealth | well-contented | what |
| wealth | well-refined | what |
| wealth | well-seeing | what |
| wealth | well-tuned | what |
| wealth | went | what |
| wear | were | what |
| wear | were | what |
| wear | were | what |
| weary | were | what |
| weary | were | what |
| weary | were | what |
| weary | were | what |
| weed | were | what |
| weed | were | what |
| weed | were | what |
| weeds | were | what |
| weeds | were | what |
| weeds | were | what |
| weeds | were | what |
| weeks | were | what |
| weep | were | what |
| weep | were | what |
| weep | were | what |
| weigh | were | what |
| weighs | were | what |
| weight | were | what |
| welcome | were | what |
| welcome | were | what |
| welfare | were | what |
| well | were | what |
| well | were | what |
| well | were | what |
| well | were | what |
| well | were | what |
| well | were | what |
| well | wert | what |
| well | wert | what |
| well | wert | what |
| well | west | what |

what
what
what
what
what
what
what
what
what
what
what
what
what
what
what
what
what
what
what
what
what
what
whate’er
whate’er
what’s
what’s
what’s
whatsoever
when
when
when
when
when
when
when
when
when
when
when
when
when
when
when
when
when
when
when
when
when
when
when
when
when
when
when
when
when
when
when
when
when
when
when
when
when
when
when
when
when
when
when
when
when
when
when
when
when
when
when
when
when
when
when
when
when
when
when
when
when
when
when
when
when
when
when
when
when
when
when
when
when
when
when
when
when
when
when
when
when
when
when
when
when
when
when
when
when
when
when
when
when
when
when
when
when
when
when
when
when
when
when
when
when
when
when
when
when
when
when
whenas
whence
whence
whence
whe’r
where
where
where
where
where
where
where
where
where
where
where
where
where
where
where

| | | |
|---|---|---|
| where | which | which |
| where | which | which |
| where | which | which |
| where | which | which |
| where | which | which |
| where | which | which |
| where | which | which |
| where | which | which |
| where | which | which |
| where | which | which |
| where | which | which |
| where | which | which |
| where | which | which |
| where | which | which |
| where | which | which |
| where | which | which |
| where | which | which |
| where | which | which |
| where | which | which |
| where | which | which |
| where | which | which |
| where | which | which |
| wherefore | which | which |
| wherefore | which | which |
| wherefore | which | which |
| wherefore | which | which |
| wherein | which | which |
| wherein | which | which |
| wherein | which | which |
| wherein | which | which |
| wherein | which | which |
| whereof | which | which |
| whereof | which | which |
| whereon | which | which |
| whereon | which | which |
| whereon | which | which |
| where-through | which | which |
| whereto | which | which |
| whereto | which | which |
| whereto | which | which |
| whereupon | which | which |
| wherever | which | which |
| wherewith | which | which |
| whether | which | which |
| whether | which | which |
| whether | which | which |
| whether | which | which |
| whether | which | which |
| whether | which | which |
| which | which | which |
| which | which | which |

which
which
which
which
while
while
while
while
while
while
while
whilst
whilst
whilst
whilst
whilst
whilst
whilst
whilst
whilst
whilst
whilst
whilst
whit
white
white
white
white
white
white
white
who
who
who
who
who
who
who
who
who
who
who
who
who
who
who
who
who
who
who
who
who
who
who
who
who
who
who
who
who
who
whoever
whole
whom
whom
whom
whom
whom
whom
whom
whom
whom
whom
whom
whom
who's
whose
whose
whose
whose
whose
whose
whose
whose
whose
whose
whose
whose
whose
whose
whose
whose
whose
whose
whose
why
why
why
why
why
why
why
why
why
why
why
why
why
why
why
why
why
why
why
why
why
why
why
why
why
wide
wide
wide
wide
wide
wide
wide
widow
widow
widow'd
widow's
wife
wights
wild
wilful
wilful
wilfully
wilfulness
Will
Will
Will
Will
Will
will
will
will
will
will
will
will
will
will
will

will
will
will
will
will
will
will
will
will
will
will
will
will
will
will
will
will
will
will
will
will
will
will
will
will
will
will
will
will
will
will
will
will
will
will
will
will
will
will
will
will
will
will
will
will
will
will
will
will
willing
willing
willingly
wills
wills
wilt
wilt
wilt
wilt
wilt
wilt
wilt
wilt
wilt
wilt
wilt
wilt
wilt
wilt
win
win
win
win
wind
wind
windows
windows
windows
winds
winds
windy
wing
winged
wink
wink
winter
winter
winter
winter
winter
winter's
winter's
winter's
winters
winters'
wires
wires
wiry
wisdom
wise
wise
wish
wish
wish
wish
wish
wish'd
wishing
wit
wit
wit
wit
wit
wit
with
with
with
with
with
with
with
with
with
with
with
with
with
with
with
with
with
with
with
with
with
with
with
with
with
with
with
with
with
with
with
with
with
with
with
with
with
with
with
with

with
with
with
with
with
with
with
with
with
with
with
with
with
with
with
with
with
with
with
with
with
with
with
with
with
with
with
with
with
with
with
with
with
with
with
with
with
with
with
with
with
with
with
with
with
with
with
with
with
with
with
with
with
with
with
with
with
with
with
with
with
with
with
with
with
with
with
with
with
with
with
with
with
with
with
with
with
with
with
with
with
with
with
with
with
with
with
with
with
with
with
with
with
with
with
with
with
with
with
with
with
with
with
with
with
with
with
with
with
with
with
with
with
with
with
with
with
with
with
with
with
with
with
with
with
with
with
with
with
with
with
with
with
with
with
with
with
with
with
with
with
with
with
with
with
withal
withering
within
within
within
within
within
within
within
within
within
within

within
without
without
without
without
without
without
without
without
witness
witness
witness
wits
wits
woe
woe
woe
woe
woe
woe
woe
woe
woe
woe
woe
woe
woeful
woes
wolf
woman
woman
woman
woman's
woman's
woman's
womb
womb
wombs
women's
women's
women's
won
wonder
wonder
wonder
wondering
wondrous
wondrous
wont
woo
woo'd
wood
wood
wood's
wooing
woos
word
word
words
words
words
words
words
words
words
words
words
words
work
work
work
workings
work's
works
works
works
world
world
world
world
world
world
world
world
world
world
world
world
world
world
world
world
world
world
world
world
world
world
world
world
world
world
world
world
world's
world's
world's
world's
world's
world-without-
end
worms
worms
worms
worms
worse
worse
worse
worse
worse
worser
worship
worst
worst
worst
worst
worst
worst
worst
worth
worth
worth
worth
worth
worth
worth
worth
worth
worth
worth
worth
worth
worth
worth
worth
worth
worth
worth
worth
worthier
worthiness
worthless
worthless
worth's
worths
worthy

worthy
worthy
worthy
worthy
would
would
would
would
would
would
would
would
would
would
would
would
would
would
would
would
would
would
would
would
would
wouldst
wouldst
wouldst
wound
wound
wound
wound
wounded
wrack
wrackful
wreck'd
wretch
wretch
wretched
wretched
wretched
wretched
wretch's
wrinkle
wrinkles
wrinkles
wrinkles
wrinkles
wrinkles
writ
writ
writ
writ
writ
writ
write
write
write
write
write
write
write
write
write
write
writers
writes
written
wrong
wrong
wrong
wrong
wrong
wrong
wrongfully
wrongs
wrongs
wrought
wrought

ye
ye
yea
year
year
year
year
years
years
years
yellow
yellow
yellow'd
yet
yet
yet
yet
yet
yet
yet
yet
yet
yet
yet
yet
yet
yet
yet
yet
yet
yet
yet
yet
yet
yet
yet
yet
yet
yet
yet
yet
yet
yet
yet
yet
yet
yet
yet
yet
yet
yet
yet
yet
yet
yet
yet
yet
yet
yet
yet
yield
yield
yore
you
you
you
you
you
you

you
you
you
you
you
you
you
you
you
you
you
you
you
you
you
you
you
you
you
you
you
you
you
you
you
you
you
you
you
you
you
you
you
you
you
you
you
you
you
you
you
you
you
you
you
you
you
you
you
you
you

you
you
you
you
you
you
you
you
you
you
you
you
you
you
you
you
you
you
you
you
you
you
you
you
you
you
you
you
you
you
you
you
you
you
you
you
you
you
you
you
you
you
you
you
you
you
you
you
you
you
you

you
you
you
you
you
young
young
young
young
youngly
your
your
your
your
your
your
your
your
your
your
your
your
your
your
your
your
your
your
your
your
your
your
your
your
your
your
your
your
your
your
your
your
your
your
your
your
your
your
your
your
your

your
your
your
your
your
your
your
your
your
your
your
your
your
your
your
your
your
your
your
your
your
your
your
your
your
your
your
your
your
your
your
your
your
your
your
your
your
your
your
your
your
your
your
your
your
your
your
yours
yours
yours
yours
yours
yourself
yourself
yourself
yourself
yourself
yourself
yourself
yourself
yourself
yourself
yourself
yourself's
youth
youth
youth
youth
youth
youth
youth
youth
youth
youth
youth
youth
youth
youth
youth
youthful
youthful
youth's

zealous

# ACKNOWLEDGEMENTS

Heartfelt thanks to Teresa Carmody and Vanessa Place, Annette Gilbert, Vivien Knussi, and Klaus Killisch, Michalis Pichler, Emma Williams and Elizabeth Hall for their contributions, efforts, comments, encouragement, and patience.

This book is for Iris.

**Mark Rutkoski** is an artist working in various media including sound and words. He has exhibited his work in New York and the UK. Paintings from his series based upon *Finnegans Wake* illustrated the October 1984 issue of the *James Joyce Broadsheet* (University of Leeds, UK). Other book projects in progress are *Definitions of* Ludwig Wittgenstein's *Remarks on Color; Last Words*, a chapbook extracted from Samuel Beckett's *Texts for Nothing*; and the *Unsung Cantos of Ezra Pound*. He lives in New York City.

**Annette Gilbert** is a postdoctoral Dilthey Fellow at Peter Szondi Institute of Comparative Literature at Freie Universität Berlin. Her current research interests include: aesthetics, experimental literature and art, interart studies, concept art / conceptual writing, and artists' books. Her anthology *Re-Print. Appropriation (&) Literature* will be published by luxbooks in 2012.

**Klaus Killisch** studied painting at the Art Academy in East-Berlin from 1981-1986. His work has been represented in many exhibitions including the Biennale in Venice, Sezon Museum of Art in Tokyo, Folkwang Museum in Essen, New National Gallery in Berlin, Museum of Contemporary Art Frankfurt / Oder. Killisch lives in Berlin. <http://www.magnetberg.de>

**Vivien Knussi** is an art historian who teaches at Pratt Institute in Brooklyn. Her field of specialization is contemporary photography. She also works as an art consultant in New York.

LES FIGUES PRESS

Post Office Box 7736
Los Angeles, CA 90007
www.lesfigues.com